Best wishes —
Dick Hillman

Glover Steam Locomotives
The South's Last Steam Builder

The Douglass was shipped from Glover on September 17, 1904.

Acknowledgments

This book exists because of the Glover family. It exists not only because of the incredible job they have done preserving their heritage through generations, it exists because of their generosity in sharing their heritage with me. "Bo" and Jim Glover were very patient with my never-ending questions and my constant digging in the Glover archives. My sincere thanks to you both.

Thanks also to Martin O'Toole and Dave Lathrop whose skill and good humor made the 18-month-long photo processing job both possible and enjoyable. At the heart of this work are the photographs, and their contribution in that regard is significant. While on the subject of photographs, I would be remiss if I did not acknowledge Eastman Kodak for their incredible generosity in providing the supplies necessary for production of the contact prints.

And last, thanks to my wife Cynthia, who put up with a lot of disruption and spousal absences and responded to my frequent pleas for word processing assistance.

Richard L. Hillman

Library of Congress Catalog Card Number 94-94146
ISBN: 0-911581-40-5
First Edition
Printed in the United States of America

HEIMBURGER HOUSE PUBLISHING COMPANY
7236 West Madison Street
Forest Park, Illinois 60130

©1996 Heimburger House Publishing Co., Forest Park, Illinois. All rights reserved. Nothing may be reprinted or copied in any manner, in whole or part, without the express written permission from the Publisher.

Table Of Contents

Foreword 4	**Chapter 6** The Biggest and the Fewest 44
Chapter 1 The Glovers Come to Georgia 8	**Chapter 7** Photo Gallery .... Littlest ...... 48 Middleweights ..... 57 Biggest 85
Chapter 2 The Glover Complex 18	**Chapter 8** Puzzle Pages 103
Chapter 3 The Glover Locomotives 28	Epilogue 110
Chapter 4 The Littlest Glovers 32	Locomotive Roster 111
Chapter 5 The Glover Middleweights 38	Index 128

The crew at the Glover plant; date is unknown.

Foreword

A chain of circumstances in the summer of 1990 led to my first acquaintance with the Glover family of Marietta, Georgia and their wonderful old company with its colorful past.

As I became acquainted with James Bolan Glover IV, and his son, Jim, they shared with me a dream they had of restoring one of the three Glover-built steam locomotives still in the old foundry building. I knew their dream to memorialize Marietta's role as a builder of locomotives could be realized with help from the right people. Today, Glover-built locomotive #81421 sits on display alongside the CSX main line in downtown Marietta, across the tracks from the old NC&StL depot.

In the process of getting the little Glover engine restored, I carefully reviewed the old records that were still available from the locomotive production years, including what originally was a collection of 931 glass plate negatives. Devising a means of printing the entire collection of negatives became a top priority. Over the years, 78 of these plates had disappeared, and of the 853 left, many had deteriorated or cracked, making them of little use. Also included in the 853 plates were repetitive photos and photos of the pipe fittings the company produced.

761 RELEVANT PLATES

A total of 92 poor quality, repetitive photos or photos of pipe castings were not selected for printing, leaving a collection of 761 plates relevant to the locomotive production years. This is remarkable considering Glover built about 200 locomotives!

When we looked for an affordable means to make prints from 761 glass plate negatives, we were confronted with a serious financial problem. Eastman Kodak was contacted about the collection, and advised that contact prints should be made before further deterioration of the plates took place. They were so committed to this preservation project that they donated the necessary supplies to ensure its completion.

It took us 18 months, during which time my basement windows were sealed with black plastic, and a large portion of the basement devoted to a mass production darkroom, but the task was completed, thanks to the untiring efforts of Martin K. O'Toole and David Lathrop, plus a host of friends pressed into darkroom work service.

906

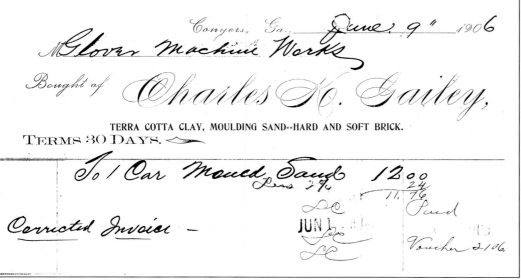

A large portion of this book is devoted to the many photographs reproduced from these glass plates. I think you will be surprised at many of these photographs, because while the Glovers tried to emulate the big locomotive builders by producing builders' photos, they were, nonetheless, a relatively small family enterprise in the rural South. Their builder's photos reflect this with the frequent inclusion of grandchildren, dogs—and women with Carmen Miranda hats. This is not surprising when you understand that J.B. Glover was operating the camera. To me, that makes these photos unique and gives them a charm all their own. I wonder how many Baldwin builders photos were taken by Mathias W. Baldwin?

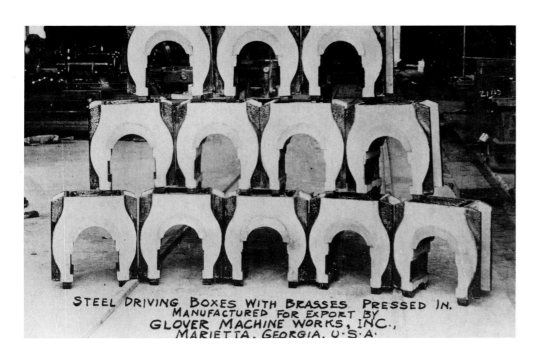

STEEL DRIVING BOXES WITH BRASSES PRESSED IN.
MANUFACTURED FOR EXPORT BY
GLOVER MACHINE WORKS, INC.,
MARIETTA, GEORGIA, U.S.A.

SHARE THE INFORMATION

The overwhelming amount of material the Glovers preserved, along with the opportunity to review the material in depth, resulted in the urge to share this information. There have been previous articles on Glover locomotives published prior to this undertaking and credit is given to Mallory Hope Ferrell, Alton Lanier, Tom Lawson and others who have written material giving us the opportunity to better understand the Glover Machine Works and its fascinating products. However, this is the first time an in-depth study could be conducted and a more complete and accurate record of these locomotives created.

The locomotive output of the Glover Machine Works never came close to that of the major builders such as American, Baldwin or Porter. For most of the 100 year existence of the company, the focus was on the production of products other than locomotives. But build them they did, and that puts the Glover name on that important list of the Steam Locomotive Builders of America.

James Bolan Glover, II

Chapter 1
The Glovers Come to Georgia

Armed conflict has always produced sweeping changes throughout the fabric of humanity, and so it was in America during the War Between the States. The war years, with the tremendous demand for products with which the war was fought, saw dramatic changes in the industrialization of America. Because of the strong predominance of agriculture and lack of industrial development in the South, the war years and those immediately following were years of particularly dramatic change. These painful, exciting and colorful times are documented in records of the Glover Machine Works of Marietta, Georgia.

John Heyward Glover, Jr. arrived in Georgia in 1848 from South Carolina. His first enterprise was a tannery that ultimately became engaged in the production of shoes for the Confederate Army. When General William Tecumseh Sherman arrived in Marietta on his well-publicized march through the South, he took a dim view of the efforts of the Glovers with predictable results.

James Bolan Glover, IV   **James Bolan Glover, V**

At the conclusion of hostilities, the Glovers had the opportunity to start another business, and the next family-operated enterprise was the result of the purchase of an existing machine shop acquired in 1888 by James Bolan Glover, II, grandson of John Heyward Glover, Jr., who was 22 years old at the time. Sadly, he saw his new enterprise prosper for only 11 years, dying in 1897 at 33 years of age. The Glovers' entry into the machine shop business reflects the very early beginnings of America's changing economy, and especially the South's, as the country began its shift toward an industrial-based society.

GLOVERS SEE FUTURE

The Glovers could see the future. By 1892, the machine shop proudly carried the Glover name, and some of the early products reflected the growth areas of turn-of-the-century America. The demand for lumber was felt all over the United States and

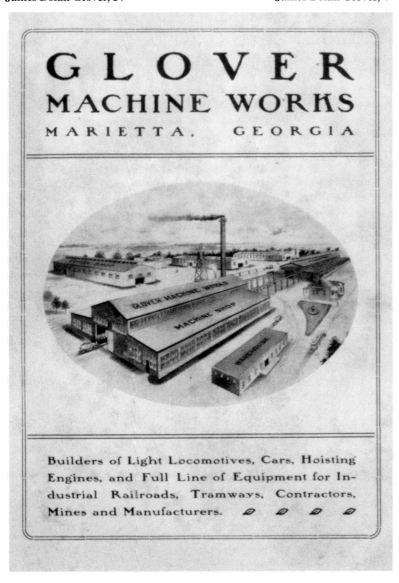

Glover hoisting machine.

A newly-manufactured log skidder is being check out prior to delivery to a customer.

A painted log skidder sits among partially-completed steam locomotives.

especially in the South with the proliferation of the ever-popular pine tree, plus cedar from the South's swampy areas, and the Glovers saw an opportunity.

One of their earliest and most popular products was a steam-powered log skidder. This device was, simply, a steam-powered winch with a vertical boiler that provided a woods crew with the means to drag huge logs out of otherwise inaccessible areas, and

Inside the Glover plant there were all types of milling machines, lathes, grinders and drills. A portion of a log skidder is shown.

Double cylinder single-drum link-motion engines as in the Glover catalog.

then by means of a derrick apparatus, convert the "skidder" to a "loader."

As the logging industry grew, so did the need for loggers to reach farther into the forests. At the same time, growth was also impacting other areas of America's industrial scene, namely the mining and quarry industries, and the Glovers participated in those industries along with the lumber industry. The

Glover files have numerous drawings and photographs of marble polishing machines and quarry derricks that they produced. At the turn of the century the United States was in the midst of a building boom. The archives of the Glover Machine Works is an amazing window through which one can look back and see these changes. One of the major ways that growth impacted the Glover Machine Works was when their customers inquired about the availability of steam locomotives. Again, the Glovers saw an opportunity. The records reveal the first Glover-built locomotive rolled out the doors of their shop in 1902. This tiny 36" gauge 0-4-0 tank locomotive with builder's #8141 was shipped to the Stratton Brick Company of Macon, Georgia on May 6 of that year.

ORDERS PEAK IN 1917

The steady growth of locomotive production over the ensuing years parallels growth of the lumbering

An employee leans against the large marble polishing table inside the Glover plant in the very early days. Note the overhead belts that power machinery.

and mining industries in the South, with locomotive orders peaking between 1910 and 1917. In 1917 alone, the Glover Machine Works produced 16 locomotives. A serious decline in production began after 1920, when the company received orders for 12 units. In 1922, only two locomotives were built and 10 more were built over the last eight years of pro-

Quarry cranes, such as this one located at a marble quarry, were also made by Glover. Marble quarries were located within easy reach of the Glover plant. 406

duction. One engine was built and shipped in 1930, builder's #101440, leaving the Marietta shops on Georgia Railroad flat car #12015 on April 19 of that year, consigned to the Chattahoochee Brick Co. of Chattahoochee, Georgia.

By 1930, the Glovers had begun casting and machining a wide variety of products and even continue to this day, with the bulk of business in the production of high pressure pipeline components.

The years of steam locomotive production are a treasured part of the history of the Glover Machine Works, and the family prides itself on its participation in a colorful and productive chapter of the industrial development of the South. In addition to the glass plate negatives, locomotive drawings and blueprints exist, as does an enormous inventory of hardwood patterns from which all the locomotive parts were cast, including engine frames. Even the camera that took the original photographs contained in this book was stored in the archives.

It has been said, and quoted that, "One could order a Glover locomotive even today and Glover could build it." Sadly, that is not true. While a tremendous amount of required information and material is available, many necessary ingredients are not. Much of the equipment and tooling has been dispersed. The Glovers never did made their own boilers, and the Glover personnel who knew how to build these machines are long gone. It is true, however, that by virtue of having so many priceless patterns, locomotive parts can be made.

Because so much of the Glover locomotive history remains in place, close examination of their locomotive production years is possible. We will look at the facility from where these machines came, look at the records that have been preserved, and examine the machines that carried the Glover name throughout the United States and several foreign countries.

Apparently, a load of machinery was being transported to Australia from the plant. 413

The frame of a steam locomotive tender being built at the Glover plant. 204

The pony truck of a Glover-built steam locomotive. 746

GLOVER MACHINE WORKS
MARIETTA, GEORGIA, U. S. A.
MANUFACTURERS OF
CAST STEEL PIPE FITTINGS

807

Harris Foundry & Machine Co.
FOUNDERS — MACHINISTS
HYDRAULIC WHEEL PRESSES
FOR HAND AND BELT POWER
REPAIRS TO ALL KINDS OF MACHINERY
MILL SUPPLIES

Cordele, Ga.

April 20th, 1937.

Glover Machine Works,
Marietta, Ga.

              Attention Mr. J. B. Glover.

Gentlemen:

    We have your inquiry of the 17th inst., for quotation on boiler tubes, and regret to advise that we are not in position to make you a competetive price on these. We thank you, however, for the opportunity afforded us to quote on same.

          Yours very truly,
          HARRIS FOUNDRY & MACHINE CO.,
                        President.

RRH/PC

Edward Hines Lumber Co.
Lincoln St. South of Blue Island Ave.
Chicago, Ill.

Edward Hines, Pres't
L.L. Barth, Vice Pres't
C.F. Wiehe, Sec'y

Dec. 7, 1904

SUBJECT:

Glover Machine Works,
    Marietta, Ga.

Dear Sirs:

    Replying to yours of the 30th ult. It is very indefinite at the present when we will operate our recent purchases of timber in the South, perhaps not for two or three years hence; therefore will not be in the market for your line of goods for some time to come.

          Very truly yours,
          EDWARD HINES LUMBER CO.

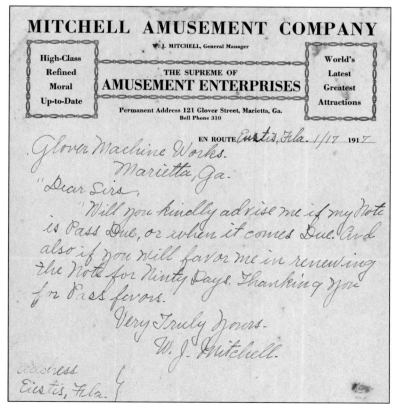

MITCHELL AMUSEMENT COMPANY
W. J. MITCHELL, General Manager
THE SUPREME OF AMUSEMENT ENTERPRISES
High-Class Refined Moral Up-to-Date
World's Latest Greatest Attractions
Permanent Address 121 Glover Street, Marietta, Ga.
Bell Phone 310

EN ROUTE Eustis, Fla. 1/17 1917

Glover Machine Works,
Marietta, Ga.

"Dear Sirs,
"Will you kindly advise me if my Note is Pass Due, or when it comes Due. And also if you will favor me in renewing the Note for Ninty Days. Thanking You for Pass favors.
    Very Truly Yours,
    W. J. Mitchell

Address Eustis, Fla.

THE EDNA BRASS MFG. CO.
HIGH-GRADE BRONZE ALLOY CASTINGS
LOCOMOTIVE APPLIANCES
LUBRICATING EQUIPMENT
STEAM SPECIALTIES

CINCINNATI, OHIO

April 2, 1940

Glover Machine Works, Inc.
Marietta, Georgia

Gentlemen:

We have your letter of March 30 in regards to the sight feed glasses furnished on your order No. 44884 and wish to advise you that the certification, as outlined in your letter, is correct and can be given without any changes.

Desiring to be of service at all times, we remain,

          Very truly yours,
          THE EDNA BRASS MFG. CO.
          Carl W. Koeppe
               Secretary

CWK:L

THE Star Head Light Co.

MANUFACTURERS OF HEAD LIGHTS. RAILROAD SIGNAL LAMPS & LANTERNS

FOR LOCOMOTIVES, CABLE & ELECTRIC CARS, AUTOMOBILES
OIL, ELECTRIC AND ACETYLENE GAS.

CABLE ADDRESS
"STARLIGHT" ROCHESTER
CODES USED
A B C
AND
LIEBERS FOURTH EDITION

ALBERT W. JACOBS,
Prest & Treas.
ALBERT W. JACK,
Vice Prest.
C. L. JACOBS,
Secretary.

COMMERCIAL ST. cor JONES ST.

Rochester, N.Y., U.S.A. Sept. 18, 06 /10

Glover Machine Works,
Marietta,, Ga.

Gentlemen:-

We enclose herewith, statement of your account, which is long overdue. This amount was for six Cab Lamps and two Marker Lamps, which we shipped on May 26th in accordance with you order 493, signed by Leon Commerford.

Will you kindly have Auditor's voucher for this small amount sent to us, and very much oblige,

Yours very truly,
STAR HEAD LIGHT CO.

AWJ/ET.

A W Jacobs
PRESIDENT

WE DO NOT BELONG TO THE HEAD LIGHT TRUST.

ALL CONTRACTS OR AGREEMENTS TO DELIVER OUR PRODUCTS CONTINGENT UPON STRIKES, ACCIDENTS AND OTHER UNAVOIDABLE DELAYS BEYOND OUR CONTROL.

JOHN P. WILLIAMS, PRESIDENT
J M OVERTON, VICE PREST AND GENL MGR
W C DIBRELL, TREASURER
C COOPER, SECRETARY

BON AIR COAL & IRON COMPANY.

PIG IRON, COAL AND COKE.

COLLIERIES
BON AIR, RAVENSCROFT AND EASTLAND
WHITE AND CUMBERLAND COUNTIES TENN.
FURNACE AND FOUNDRY COKE.

FURNACES
ALLENS CREEK, WAYNE COUNTY TENN.
"MANNIE"
EXTRA FLUID SOFTENER
SILICON AS DESIRED
"WAYNE" AND "BON AIR"
STANDARD FOUNDRY PIG.

ARCADE BUILDING.

Nashville, Tenn. Dec. 19, 1904

Glover Machine Works,
Marietta, Ga.

Gentlemen:-

Referring to yours of Dec. 14th, in reference to a small locomotive for handling our larry cars, beg to say that we have decided not to purchase the locomotive to begin with, as it will be cheaper for us to handle them by mule power until we have a larger number in service, which will probably not be before next summer. When we are in the market we will give you ample time to figure on the same, and allow for the building, after the order is given.

Yours truly,

J M Overton
General Manager.

Uniform Bill of Lading— Standard form of Straight Bill of Lading approved by the Interstate Commerce Commission by Order No. 787 of June 27, 1908

CINCINNATI, FLEMINGSBURG & SOUTHEASTERN RAILWAY CO.

STRAIGHT BILL OF LADING—ORIGINAL—NOT NEGOTIABLE.

SHIPPERS NO. _____
AGENTS NO. _____

RECEIVED, subject to the classifications and tariffs in effect on the date of issue of this Original Bill of Lading,

At FLEMINGSBURG, KENTUCKY, Sep 11th 190 9

from C F & S RR Co the property described below, in apparent good order, except as noted (contents and condition of contents of packages unknown.) marked, consigned and destined as indicated below, which said Company agrees to carry to its usual place of delivery at said destination, if on its road, otherwise to deliver to another carrier on the route to said destination. It is mutually agreed, as to each carrier of all or any of said property over all or any portion of said route to destination, and as to each party at any time interested in all or any of said property, that every service to be performed hereunder shall be subject to all the conditions, whether printed or written, herein contained (including conditions on back hereof,) and which are agreed to by the shipper, and accepted for himself and his assigns.

The Rate of Freight from Johnson to Marietta Ga is in Cents per 100 Lbs.

IF Times 1st	IF 1st Class	IF 2d Class	IF Rule 25	IF 3d Class	IF Rule 26	IF Rule 28	IF 4th Class	IF 5th Class	IF 6th Class	IF Special per 100	IF Special per
										48	

Consigned to Georgia Locomotive Co. c/o Glover Mach Works (Mail Address—Not For purpose of Delivery)
Destination Marietta State of Ga County of _____
Route L & N Car Initial _____ Car No. _____

NO. PACKAGES	DESCRIPTION OF ARTICLES AND SPECIAL MARKS	WEIGHT Subject to Correction	Class or Rate	Check Column	
1	N. G. Locomotive Eng 2039	30000			If charges are to be prepaid, write or stamp here, "To be Prepaid"
1	" " 2403?	30000			
2	" Tanks 2191	20000			
3	Bx Eng Parts				Received $_____ to apply in prepayment of the charges on the property described hereon
3	" Brass Pipe				
1	Air Pump } For Free in Way Car				_____ Agent or Cashier.
					Per _____
					(The signature here acknowledges only the amount prepaid)
					Charges Advanced: $_____

_____, Shipper Geo Faulkner Agent

Per _____ Per _____

(This Bill of Lading is to be signed by the shipper and agent of the carrier issuing same.)

Chapter 2
The Glover Complex

Back-Truck Rear-Tank Four-Driver Locomotive.

Before we take a close look at the Glover locomotives, let's look at the Glover plant. The Glovers entered the machine shop business in 1888 by purchasing an existing business known as the Phoenix Foundry and Machine Shop, operated by the Withers family. This business was located immediately to the west of the Western & Atlantic Railroad and south of Whitlock Avenue in downtown Marietta.

In order to meet the growing need for the products and services of their machine shop, the business was moved to a new 11 acre site in 1903. A 1905 Sanborn insurance map shows the complex as originally developed. It has been documented that the first Glover steam locomotive was delivered in 1902, meaning that at least one, and possibly as many as four engines were produced at the earlier location.

NEW LOCATION

The new location was developed in response to what the Glovers saw as a growing part of their enterprise, with a 435' long by 100' wide foundry and erecting hall complex designed and built to efficiently handle large products such as skidders and locomotives. The foundry and erecting hall presented the appearance of a single structure, but it was actually

The science building under construction c. 1927

The science building under construction c. 1927

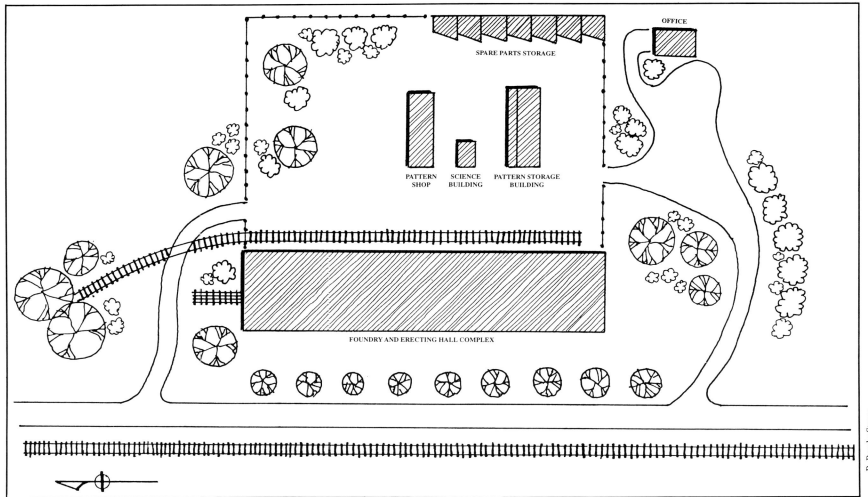

Glover complex as it appeared in 1995.

Undated catalog believed to have been issued c. 1916-1919.

built as two separate buildings, with the south end of the complex the foundry, separated by an open area connected to the north machining and erecting area only by the overhead crane rails. Enclosing of the complex into one long structure occurred around 1927. A 1923 Sanborn insurance map shows the separate buildings as originally developed. The main building in the complex is essentially on a north-south axis and parallel to the Western & Atlantic main line and separated from the same by Butler Street.

At the far north end of the property, a siding runs from the W&A into what is known today as Butler Street Yard, with the siding continuing from the south end of the yard across Butler Street and into the Glover property. On the Glover property, a switch permits movement into or out of the north end of the main building or onto a track that ran the entire length of the east side of the main building. This east siding enabled rail cars of sand to be placed adjacent to huge doors through which the sand was off loaded. The sand was stored in sand bays then utilized for the casting process in the extreme south end of the building.

Frame of incomplete locomotive still in plant in 1995.

The product flow was from the casting of parts at the south end, to the gradual assembly of the locomotives as the various parts and sub-assemblies moved north, to the final assembly in the north end of the building, and finally out doors at the north end and onto tracks of the W&A.

To facilitate handling of the variety of gauges of locomotives built, four rails were eventually installed in the floor of the erecting hall and out the north doors. These rails were in gauges of 24", 36" and standard gauge of 4' 8 1/2".

PATTERN SHOP

At a distance of 30 yards east of the foundry building were three separate buildings built parallel to one another, perpendicular to the foundry building, and on an east-west axis. The northern most of the three was a 30' x 90' frame building. It was the pattern shop where highly skilled craftsmen turned blueprints of locomotive parts into hardwood patterns. These patterns were made from a variety of hardwoods such as maple and cherry. Patterns were often made from several different types of woods, resulting in fascinating colors and wood grains. The hardness of the wood was dependent upon the complexity of the shape needing to be duplicated, with the hardest woods such as oak utilized for simple shapes and softer woods used for more complex shapes.

Drawings or blueprints used by patternmakers came from the next building. Thirty feet to the south of the pattern shop stood a two-story brick structure built around 1927 which measured 20' x 32'. It housed a laboratory on the first floor where chemical and metallurgical studies were performed. The second floor was devoted to drafting and blueprint operations. This sturdy building eventually housed the Glover archives.

Immediately to the south of the "science" building was a 30' x 96' frame building, originally a single story building with a second floor added later. This structure was about 30' from the lab building and had a simple shed roof added to its north side under which a variety of fascinating motor vehicles were stored including a 1920s era Lafayette and a pair of early 1950s Hudson coupes. This building was the pattern storage area. Once a pattern was produced in the pattern shop, it was entered into a pattern log and then stored in the pattern building for future use. When a specific part was needed, the pattern was retrieved, taken to the foundry where it was packed into sand, carefully removed, and the impression it left filled with molten metal.

The Glover complex as it appeared in 1995 just prior to demolition. The view is to the northeast.

Exterior and interior views of the science building.

23

The two-story pattern building holds the numerous wood locomotive patterns.

Interior of pattern storage building.

Tool and fixture rack in the foundry/machine shop.

SPARE PARTS STORAGE

Often many parts were made while the pattern was out, and the plant was set up to make the particular part. These spare parts were inventoried for future use in a set of six saw-toothed roofed, brick structures adjoining one another about 60' behind the pattern storage, lab and pattern shop buildings. These buildings, about 30' x 30', provided natural light through skylight windows. They contained large racks where parts reposed for future use, and they were also used for pattern storage overflow.

The amount of patterns stored in several of the Glover buildings was amazing. Realizing that so many of the hundreds of parts in a locomotive start as a piece of wood from which the final part is made, and that the Glovers saved virtually all of these patterns, it's easy to understand the importance of this collection.

Robert Johnson, an historic preservation consultant who has researched other locomotive builders' records, has assessed the Glover facility. He says, "Glover's patterns are practically unique in preservation, in that the patterns from the better-known locomotive producers such as American, Baldwin, and Lima, are virtually gone. Nowhere but at the Glover facility can sets of patterns be found to build a locomotive." Johnson further states, "Glover, at this date of writing, has an unparalleled archive of its historic records in all categories." The amount of material in the archives is overwhelming. It has taken an incredible amount of time to work through the material to unearth answers to specific questions. For example, information is yet to be found relative to used locomotives that the Glovers accepted as trade-ins.

CONSTRUCTION SPECS

One of the most complete and interesting records of the locomotives is contained in large format, 9" x 14" string-bound binders containing construction specifications for each cylinder size locomotive. Each size has its own binder in builder's number sequence, and many contain a copy of the builder's photo glued to the first page. These binders also contain a label glued to the inside of the cover that provides stern instructions as to how the binder is to be used.

Complementing the photographic record of the Glover locomotives is a set of correspondence files for each locomotive, along with photographs and construction data that presents a very complete story on each locomotive. These files generally begin with a letter or telegram from a potential customer inquiring about the price and availability of a locomotive. Then the files continue through a formal proposal from the Glovers, containing specifications of the engine and quoting the price, delivery date and terms of sale.

Once the proposal was accepted via the customer's signature, the files continued on with the usual "hurry-up" letters from the customer, followed by letters from the Glovers trying to explain some unforeseen delay. Incidentally, not all of the Glover's proposals met with success, as evidenced by a letter from a prospective customer advising the Glovers that, rather than purchase a locomotive, they would get the job done with a mule. The last item often found in the construction sequence of the locomotive was a copy of the Hartford boiler inspection certificate. And then, finally, we find a copy of the old Western & Atlantic Railroad waybill documenting shipment of the locomotive.

Frequently there was a corresponding photo in the glass plate negative file showing the little beauty loaded on a flat car, with the flat car number referred to on the bill of lading, and the car spotted outside the north doors of the erecting hall, ready to be rolled onto the W&A main.

The flatcars carrying the Glover locomotives are, by themselves, interesting, and their photographic record is helpful and entertaining along with the locomotives. The correspondence files go into interesting dilemmas faced by the customer as he went through the shakedown phase with his new locomotive, and then into years of ordering replacement parts. Inasmuch as the files were maintained by locomotive builder's numbers and not alphabetically by the customers names, the records trace each engine through the years as they changed hands with the changing fortunes of the respective customers.

DIFFICULT TIMES

One clear and important picture that emerges is the dramatic growth of the lumber, quarry and mining industries in the first 15 or 20 years of the century, and then the rapid change and decline of many of these companies. The files are full of correspondence during the late teens and 1920s of customers having difficulty paying their indebtedness to the Glovers or their banks, of collection letters, notices of bankruptcies or buyouts. There are also notices

Labels inside of Glover binders contain stern warnings on usage.

Just a Few Glover Locomotives

One copy of this little pocket catalog was found in the files among other locomotive builders' catalogs. It has a brown card cover, with yellow title box and black type. It measures 6 1/4" x 3 1/2", consists of 25 pages similar to their other loose-leaf catalog pages except that the text is reduced in size. The title page reads *Just a Few Glover Locomotives* and there is a Foreword. The page numbers begin with #4 for the first locomotive; the illustrations are on the left and the matching specifications on the right. The illustration numbers Glover uses are printed in this catalog. The catalog is in excellent condition, was cleaned on 5/24/94 and stored in an acid-free file folder.

The catalog pages in order are: **page 4**, 4-6-0 Illustration #21, Kinder & Northwestern R.R. #101; **page 5-6**, missing; **page 7**, specifications for Mogul w/8-wheel tender, code words Rebo, Recod and Redon; **page 8-9**, 0-6-0, Illustration #16, Cleveland Oconee Lumber Co. #16, 6-wheel loco w/8-wheel tender, code words Zalen, Zomer and Zosex; **page 10-11**, 0-6-0, Illustration #18, Baum & Vanroy Crate Co. tender locomotive. This version has the wood burning stack. Code words Vope, Vocef, Vodeg, Vofec, Vog, Vores and Votex; **page 12-13**, 0-4-0, Illustration #17, J.B. Blades Lumber Co., Illustration #17, 4-wheel locomotive w/ 4-wheel tender, code words Qube, Quced, Quden, Qufeg, Qulef, Qumaf, Quman; **page 14-15**, 0-6-2, Illustration #3, A.T. Squier #4, 6-wheel locomotive with back truck and rear tank; **page 16-17**, 0-4-2, Illustration #2, Pittsburg Lumber Co., 4-wheel locomotive with 4-wheel truck and rear tank; **page 18-19**, 0-4-4, Illustration #22, Suffolk Lumber Co. #1, 4-wheel locomotive with 4-wheel truck and rear tank; **page 20-21**, 0-4-0T, Illustration #15, Alabama Fuel and Iron Co., heavy 4-wheel saddle tank locomotive; **page 22-23**, 0-4-0T, Illustration #5, Campbell Coal Co., light 4-wheel saddle tank locomotive, sizes 7x12, 8x14 & 9x14, for Leer, Legion and Lend, are in the English-Spanish catalog but this catalog adds 10x14 Lent, 10x16 Life, 11x16 Lime and 12x16 Limit; **page 24-25**, 0-6-0T, Illustration #10, T.C.I. & R.R. Co. #17, light 6-wheel saddletank locomotive, 7x12 Nag, 8x14 Nail, and 9x14 Nap.

of mysterious fires sweeping through sawmills, and locomotive repossessions. The conclusion is inescapable: they clearly and painfully document the declining fortunes of those in the lumber and mining industries in the South and the onset of the Depression years.

The Glovers issued a variety of product catalogs for locomotives as well as for skidders and pipe components. The locomotive catalogs are undated, a common practice at that time, and trying to affix a date is problematical in that many of the illustrations utilize considerable artistic license rendering the locomotives unidentifiable.

Five different types of Glover locomotive catalogs have been discovered. What appears to be the earliest catalog found is a vertical 8" x 10" loose-leaf edition showing 13 different locomotives, some of which the Glovers never built. Several of the locomotives pictured are identical to ones pictured in a Porter locomotive catalog issued sometime after 1908.

SMALLEST CATALOG

The smallest Glover catalog is a horizontal format 6 1/4" x 3 1/2" 25 page edition marked catalog "E", and based on some of the locomotives illustrated, appears to have been issued in the years between 1916-1919. The third catalog is also in a horizontal format, measuring 8" x 5 1/4" and containing 69 pages. Based on the locomotives pictured in this version, it's possible to approximate its date as the early 1920s. The fourth catalog was a bilingual English/Spanish horizontal edition of an unknown number of pages, because only one incomplete copy has been found. The fifth version is catalog "C". The smaller catalogs present a problem because they are bound issues, making changes such as deletions or additions to the locomotive lineup impossible. Catalog C is an 11 1/2" x 9" loose-leaf publication, with the cover printed in a horizontal format and the pages printed in a vertical format. No previously assembled Catalog C has been located so the exact extent of this catalog is obscure. A minimum of 35 different pages are known to exist, depicting an astonishing array of locomotives that were apparently offered.

The Glovers were locomotive builders and not merely assemblers of locomotives totally built from other manufacturers' parts, so their files include draw-

The six "saw-toothed" roofed structures at the east side of the complex were used for storage.

One of the 0-4-0 saddletank locomotives, #7128, was still in the main building until late 1995.

ings and blueprints created by their own designers and draftsmen. They include the major components such as frames and cabs down to the smallest fittings and valves. The Glovers were very early proponents of all-steel cabs, equipping their locomotives with them as early as 1906. Their trademark was curved-top side cab windows.

The Glovers outsourced many items such as headlights and gauges just like other locomotive builders, but they also built their own steam brake valve. The drawings for these components are on file. They also produced a book of replacement parts for customers showing part numbers and dimensions. This book, and other drawings, were rendered on linen paper.

The archives contain business records dating to the late 1800s. The Glovers had a sense of this and responded accordingly. Because of their desire to retain the details of their business, future generations will have the opportunity to look back and learn.

Glover locomotive #81421 today is displayed near the CSX main line in downtown Marietta, Georgia.

121631   496

28

Chapter 3
The Glover Locomotives

As requests to consider building steam locomotives increased, the Glovers were faced with an important decision. Building steam powered log skidders was one thing, but building locomotives, while similar in their propulsion, was quite another.

Contained in the Glover records are proposals and specifications from many other locomotive manufacturers, sent no doubt by potential Glover customers, to solicit a similar proposal from them. The Glovers received these requests from customers they were already doing business with, and they did not want to lose them as customers. Converting a relatively small shop with limited financial resources into a locomotive factory required considerable skill and creativity. The Glovers were in no position to attempt reinvention of the wheel, so they closely followed the larger locomotive manufacturers as they entered into the production and marketing of steam locomotives.

One manifestation of their need to emulate the older, established locomotive manufacturers is seen in comparing the illustrations from an H.K.Porter catalog and a Glover catalog. The similarities are both undeniable and understandable. The records also indicate a wise move by the Glovers to begin to repair locomotives manufactured by others. There really is no better way to fully understand the intricacies of construction of a locomotive than to rebuild one.

LOCOMOTIVES REBUILT

The few records found relating to the repair business indicate that mostly H.K.Porter units came through the shop for rebuilding, often times including a change in gauge. Some of the records indicate very fast service, with units arriving and leaving in less than two weeks. The records also indicate many trade-ins, and they no doubt required the services of the Glover shop crews to get them ready for resale.

Glover engines were built during the years 1902 to 1930 in 13 cylinder sizes and eight gauges: 24", 30", 34.8", 36", 39 3/8", 40", 42" and standard gauge of 4' 8 1/2". They categorized their engines by cylinder size, the smallest being 5" x 8", and the largest being 16 x 20". While one might assume that the larger cylinder size equates to the larger gauges, that is not necessarily so. The Glovers built some engines with very small cylinder dimensions on standard gauge frames and vice-versa.

Claims have been made down through the years that the Glovers built some 500 locomotives, but the records unearthed so far document the production of less than 200 units. However, there is no doubt that more locomotives were built than the records reveal. It is expected, for example, that some locomotives were built as "pilot projects" for which no builder's numbers were assigned. Further evidence of incomplete records is found in the glass plate negatives, where photos indicate Glover-built locomotives lettered for customers for which no other records can be found, and builder's numbers cannot be determined. There are only a few such cases, but it does make the total number of units clouded. There is no doubt, however, that the total number of units built rests at about 200.

BUILDER'S PLATES

Glover engines carry their own, unique brand of builder's numbers using a combination of cylinder size and sequence number within that cylinder size.

101429   518

The illustrations on this page show some of the locomotive photos from the Glover archives. The locomotives presumably came to the Glover plant for repair, rebuilding or resale. None of these are Glover-built units.

23

160

30 155

A unit with 8 x 14" cylinders, for example, being the first one of that cylinder size built, carried the builder's number of 8141. The first Glover builder's plates were a simple round cast disc similar to that used by Porter locomotives. This format was used until the fall of 1916, at which time the builder's plate became an attractive shield-shaped device.

Through the years the Glovers were regarded by those who were aware of these engines as builders of primarily narrow gauge engines. This reputation is inaccurate in that the records demonstrate that 53% of their production was in standard gauge. A total of 44 of their locomotives or 23% of their output was in the 12 x 16" cylinder size with the remainder scattered over the other 12 sizes. For comparison, the big main line locomotives of the major builders, such

Porter loco 489

INSPECTION CAR

as American, used cylinders that measured in the upper 20s and into the 30s, such as 26 x 32".

For such a relatively small producer of locomotives, Glover's customers were in a surprisingly wide ranging market, with locomotives being shipped to 12 foreign countries, and to 12 states within the continental United States. Most of the foreign countries that received Glover locomotives were in the Caribbean and South America, but two locomotives found their way to Russia and one to South Africa. While the southeastern part of the United States was obviously the primary Glover market, they enjoyed sales as far away as the states of Washington and California.

GLOVERS EXIST

Several Glover locomotives still exist. In addition to the #81421 on display in Marietta, two locomotives were still in the Glover foundry: #7128 and #91419. The remains of two locomotives are stored at Arigama, a museum in Tifton, Georgia. A decision regarding restoration still needs to be made. These two units are believed to be #131810 and #131812. Another locomotive is reportedly in existence in Puerto Rico where #121645 is said to survive, and another in Ecuador. One heavily modified unit, #10168, was on display outside a restaurant in Gainesville, Florida until just a few years ago when it was sold to a man from Ohio.

An even closer, more detailed look at specific locomotives is made possible by the strict policy the Glovers had of filing every piece of correspondence relating to each locomotive sold. A page by page examination of these files often reveals an interesting story, and the next three chapters are devoted to some of those stories covering the small, medium and larger Glover locomotives.

In the archives, drawings were found of items that may have been planned, but were never produced.

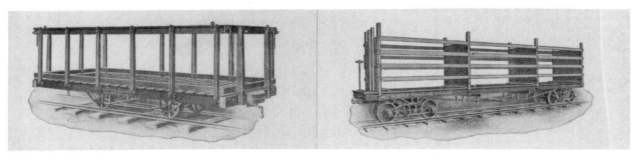

581 & 582   573

Chapter 4
The Littlest Glovers

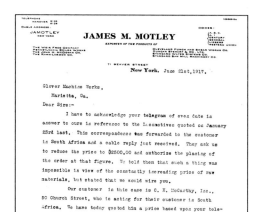

Our focus now turns to the smallest of the Glover locomotives, those built with 5 x 8", 7 x 12", 8 x 14" and 9 x 14" inch cylinders.

The photographs of locomotives #581 and #582 show just how tiny these little teakettles really were. Note the above photograph includes a couple of gentlemen, which helps relate the scale. The tops of their heads are higher than the tops of the headlights on the engines! The gentleman on the left is an unnamed boiler inspector and on the right is George Welsh, an engineer with the Glover Works. The non-traditional nature of these builder's photos gives them a unique flavor.

A letter from the Glover archives dated 1917 reveals that engine #583 most likely wound up in South Africa. This engine sold for $2,875, and the Glovers asked for a one-third down payment. The broker in this transaction, J. M. Motley, fired off a letter telling the Glovers he was authorized to put only $500 down, and that the Glovers could take it or leave it.

Motley was no diplomat, as the files repeatedly demonstrate. The 1917 letter also reflects Motley's attempt to lower the price. Motley also had an interesting requirement of the Glovers. He provided the Glovers with a supply of 4 x 8" brass plates with his name on them, and instructed the Glovers to affix the plates to any locomotive brokered by him, not unlike the Buick dealer slapping his name on the back of a newly-purchased Roadmaster.

INFORMAL APPROACH

The photograph of locomotive #584, the *Eusebia*, is interesting because this unit went to a Colombia banana plantation. It shows the company's informal approach to the science of builder's photographs. It also shows what often happens to glass plate negatives. Even cracked and with a corner missing, it's still the best photo remaining of this attractive locomotive.

Locomotive #7127 presents an enigma. The photos show a fascinating machine, and the files present a puzzle. The engine was ordered by the Samana and Santiago Railway in Santo Domingo, and its 42" gauge is consistent with the other Glover engines ordered by the S & S, #13188 and #13189. Also consistent are the road numbers, #3 for the #7127, and numbers 4 and 5 for the #13188 and #13189, but there is no record of the #7127 ever being exported. Also in the files for #7127 are orders for parts from the Reynolds Coal Company of Grafton, West Virginia which is about as far from the Dominican Republic as one can get.

The correspondence files for locomotive #7128 reveal an interesting story, but sadly a builder's photo of this engine does not exist to illustrate its history. You may recall in the section on surviving Glovers that this locomotive was still in the shop, and how it got there constitutes the story. The locomotive was shipped from Marietta in June of 1926. Note the

7127   744   584   861

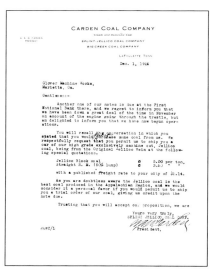

8148   370

year and recall that the files reveal customers having financial difficulty during this period. This 0-4-0T was purchased by the Splint Jellico Coal Company as their #2, and was shipped to Lafollette, Tennessee.

It was not long before dark clouds appeared on the horizon, and in August of 1926 a past due notice for payment of the locomotive arrived. In December, 1926, the Carden Coal Company, the parent of Splint-Jellico Coal Company, wrote directly to the Glovers stating that they were unable to make their payment because "the engine fell through a trestle." They conclude their letter with an attempt to barter coal for their indebtedness.

DISPATCH AGENT

After a year of negotiating, the Glovers, now out of patience, dispatched agent J. Z. Foster to repossess the engine. Foster fired off a telegram to the Glovers on December 22, 1927 to advise that he had obtained a court order to retake the engine and had rolled it off the track onto a mountain road.

A man by the name of Bell, either working for the coal company, or as an agent retained by them, was interfering with Foster's objectives. Later that same day Foster again wired the Glovers to say that he had "bought a large cable and hired a pair of mules" and that regardless of further interference from Bell, "We are pulling the engine with mules and men down the mountain." Foster continued that he had "ordered a car at the railhead to be loaded the following Saturday." On December 26, 1927 the #7128 was on its way to Marietta via the Southern Railway and the L&N, on L&N flatcar #24406. The locomotive remained with the Glovers until December, 1995 when it became the last engine to leave the plant. (See photo on dustjacket.)

In 1904, the Glovers sold locomotive #8147 to the Alabama Construction Company for $4,700 with delivery to Cartersville, Georgia. The specifications called for a 36" gauge engine with no bell and a second headlight. A photo of #8147's sister engine, #8148, shows the second headlight mounted high on the rear edge of the cab roof as a backup light. The locomotive was paid for with $1,000 down and four payments spread over a year, and the locomotive was guaranteed to haul 45 tons up a 3% grade on good track.

UNUSUAL LOCOMOTIVE

The builder's photos of locomotive #81418 depict a highly unusual locomotive with an extremely low profile. It's a little hard to believe that the low profile was designed for operation inside of a coal mine,

81418   28

and we're left to ponder the ability of the crew to breathe if that was the case. In 1917, locomotive #81418 suffered the same fate as the #7128 when the Glovers dispatched an agent to effect repossession from the Cook Jellico Coal Company. The repossession was complicated by a miner's strike, and the miners would not help the Glover's agent move the engine, nor would they allow anybody else to help. It took from August of 1917 until March of 1918 for repossession to be completed. Considering the highly unorthodox design of the locomotive it would be interesting to know what became of it.

Locomotive #81421 is the only Glover locomotive presently on public display in the United States. The #81421 was built in 1916 for the Coulbourn Brothers Lumber Co. and shipped to Emporia, Virginia on January 3, 1917. The sale price of the engine was $3,100. In 1923, the Glovers took the locomotive back, rebuilt it and offered it for resale. The Glovers received orders for only two locomotives in 1922, and several attempts to sell this locomotive failed. On October 5, 1931 the Glovers offered the locomotive to a customer in Florida for $750 and were turned down. Ersie Hamby went to work for the Glovers in 1946, retiring in 1988. Ersie told a story about the #81421 that involved one of the men he worked for at the Glover plant. Ray Pickens worked at the Glover shops during the steam locomotive construction era. After lunch, Pickens would patrol the plant collecting lunch bags and anything else that would burn

81421   542

and take them outside to where the #81421 was sitting derelict. He would throw all the material into the firebox, light it, then sit under a tree to watch the smoke curl up out of the stack until the fire went out.

MOVED INSIDE

Many years ago, and well after enough time had passed for the elements to do their best to reduce the #81421 to rust, the locomotive was finally moved inside the foundry only to virtually disappear under a pile of foundry clutter. There, in 1990, in an informal conversation with the Glovers, it was learned that a long-held dream existed with the Glovers to see this locomotive restored and placed on public display. In early 1991, the dream turned to reality as the restoration began. The work was performed by David Lathrop, an historic preservationist with a specialty in steam equipment. The work continued through most of 1991, and in June of 1992 the engine was officially unveiled. Sadly, the boiler was too badly pitted to permit safe operation of the locomotive, so it's relegated to static display, but is nonetheless restored and protected under an attractive roof. While the shed and decorative wrought iron fence provide protection for the locomotive, the fence was erected so close to the locomotive that a clear photograph of the unit is impossible.

And how appropriate that a Glover locomotive, a symbol of the enterprising spirit of the Glover family, is displayed in Marietta, because it was a Glover who became the first mayor of the city. It was also a Glover who gave the city the piece of property that became Marietta's beloved Glover Square in the heart of downtown Marietta.

GLOVER MACHINE WORKS
BUILDERS OF LIGHT LOCOMOTIVES
Marietta, Ga., U.S.A.

Specification of Tank Locomotive

FOR **Coulbourn Bros.**

TYPE **2-6-0**

SERVICE **Logging**   CODE WORD

GENERAL SPECIFICATIONS

Gauge	**3** Ft. **0** Ins.		Grate Area,		**5.4**	Sq. ft.
Cylinders,	**8** Ins diameter.		Steam Pressure,		**170**	Pounds.
	14 Ins. stroke.		Wheel Base, Driving,	**5** Ft.		Ins.
Drivers, **6** in number,	**24** Ins. diameter.		Wheel Base, Total Engine,	**10** Ft.	**6**	Ins.
Boiler. Type **Straight Top**			Wheel Base, Engine and Tender,	**23** Ft.	**0**	Ins.
Diameter,	**28** Ins.		Weights (approximately) in working order.			
Fire Box,	**26** Ins. long.		On Drivers,			Pounds.
	30 Ins. wide.		On Truck,			Pounds.
Tubes. No. **46**	**2** Ins. diameter.		Total Engine,			Pounds.
Length,	**8** Ft. **0** Ins.		Tender,			Pounds.
Heating Surface.			Tractive Power,			Pounds.
Fire box,	**30.** Sq. ft.		Fuel, **coal**	Fuel Capacity,	**3/4**	tons
Tubes,	**192.68** Sq. ft.		Water Capacity, **500**			
Total,	**222.68** Sq. ft.					

DETAILS OF CONSTRUCTION

BOILER

Type

Material — Of homogeneous open-hearth steel. Shell of best flange grade and firebox of best firebox grade.

Diameter — Diameter at front end **28** inches, at back end **28** inches.

General Construction — All parts well and thoroughly stayed. All boiler braces accurately fitted with drilled holes and turned pins secured in position by washers and cotter pins. Tube hole accurately machined to gauges, punched hole to guide cutter bar not over ¾ in. diameter to insure removal of all metal injured by punching. Fire-door openings formed by flanging and lap-riveting inside and outside sheets; tool-guard to be cast on lower part of fire-door frame. Fusible plug in crown sheet.

All longitudinal seams butt jointed with double covering plates.

Boiler Heads — Front flue sheet to have extra plate riveted above flues, making double thickness. Same on back head above fire door.

Dome — Of open-hearth steel pressed out in one piece.
Diameter, **18** inches. Height, **20** inches.
Dome ring of steel. Cap of **Cast Iron**

Thickness of Shell — Shell. Cylindrical sheets, **5/16** inches. Wagon top, **5/16** inches.
Back head, **5/16** inches. Front tube sheet, **3/8** inches.

Sheets — Throat sheet, **3/8** inches, to compensate for thinning due to flanging.

Fire Box — Of best grade firebox steel.
Length, **26** inches. Width at grates, **30** inches.
Width at top, **22** inches. Depth, **36** inches.
Thickness of sheets. Crown and sides, **5/16** inches.
Door sheet, **5/16** inch. Tube Sheet, **3/8** inch.
Water Space at front, **2** inches, at rear, **2** inches.
At sides, **2** inches. Mud ring of steel.

Tubes — Of **steel** No. **13** Wire gauge, with copper ferrules swagged at ends of firebox tube sheet.
46 in number, **2** inches diameter and **8** feet **0** inches long.

10143   141

Chapter 5
The Glover Middleweights

The middleweight locomotives covered here are locomotives with cylinders 10 x 14", 10 x 16", 11 x 16" and 12 x 16". Not surprisingly, these sizes contributed the most locomotives to the total output of the Glover Machine Works, but not by much. The 12 x 16" size was the most popular, with an output of 44 units or 23% of production. These units were built in five different gauges with standard gauge the most popular.

One of the earliest locomotives of the 10 x 14" size, the #10143, arrived on the scene courtesy of some extensive cosmetic surgery. This locomotive started life as #81411, and was shipped in June, 1906 as a standard gauge 0-6-4F. In January, 1908 it returned to the Glovers with the advice that the locomotive was too small. The customer, R.C. Avent of Moss Point, Mississippi was already using Glover locomotive #11164, and later in 1909 purchased yet another Glover, #10164.

After arriving back at the Glover works in January, 1908 the locomotive reappeared in March of the same year as #10143, still standard gauge, but now as an 0-6-0 with a four-wheeled tender. It was shipped to Munger & Bennett Lumber Company of New Bern, North Carolina, and when last heard about was working for the Mizelle Logging Company of Newport, North Carolina in 1920.

81411   360

LAST OF LOCOMOTIVES

The Chattahoochee Brick Company of Chattahoochee, Georgia (now just a part of west side Atlanta) was a regular customer of the Glovers, owning five engines. Purchased either new or used over a span of 24 years were locomotives #81410, 9145, 9148, 9149 and 101440. And, as a footnote to history provided by a satisfied customer, they purchased the last Glover-built engine of record, #101440. Records reveal the cost for the locomotive was $4,400, and it was shipped on April 19, 1930. The last piece of correspondence in the Glover archives was from 1942, when the Chattahoochee Brick Co. asked for specifications of the locomotive. By 1930, the Glovers were essentially out of the locomotive business and had abandoned their practice of photographing their engines, so their last locomotive was not photographed.

Locomotive #10168 is a special case because it is the ultimate survivor. In July, 1924 H. J. McNeill wrote to the Glovers inquiring about a locomotive, and by February 4, 1925 his new purchase was on its way. By 1928 the Edisto Hardwood Company had assumed ownership and in 1938 the third owner, Holly Hill Cypress, was operating the locomotive. The last record of the locomotive is a copy of an order for some parts dated 1954 submitted by Holly Hill who apparently was still operating it.

Interestingly, the parts order is marked "cancelled," but by whom we don't know. The locomotive then went to a park called Six Gun Territory in Florida,

CAMERON LUMBER COMPANY
MANUFACTURERS OF AND DEALERS IN LONG AND SHORT LEAF
YELLOW PINE LUMBER, ROUGH AND DRESSED
AND HARD WOOD

SMOAKS, S. C.,

H. J. MCNEILL

10168   J6 or 7

11165 22D

11165 15

then appeared as a stationary display outside the Iron Horse Restaurant in Gainesville, Florida but by this time with a modified stack and wooden cab. The restaurant folded, and the engine was purchased by Richard Stebelton of Columbus, Ohio. Stebelton managed to restore the locomotive and now operates it on his property using compressed air instead of steam.

Locomotive #11165 was one of the few Glover locomotives working in the northern part of the United States. This unit was built in 1909 for the Lane Brothers Company, a major contractor for the Ocmulgee Dam project near Jackson, Georgia. Glover glass plate #21 showing a head-on view of this locomotive is of particular interest because it clearly shows, through the open shop doors, separation of the erecting hall from the foundry building in the rear. It also reveals that in 1909 only standard gauge tracks led from the building. The dam was

> **PROPOSAL**
> **GLOVER MACHINE WORKS.**
> MARIETTA, GA.
>
> FOLIO NO._____
> PROPOSAL NO._____
>
> May 15, 1909.
>
> *1 Four wheel Saddle Tank Locomotive, Shop No.11165, now in stock. Driving Wheels 30" diamater, Cylinders 11" x 16", with the following changes as directed by Mr. C. W. Lane. Cab to be made of steel: Gauge Cocks to be of the most improved make: Lubricator, Detroit Bulls-eye pattern. Front and Back Headblocks of heavy oak, bound with steel on ends, and to be placed so that bottom will not be made of more than 4" above the top of the rail.*
>
> *Locomotive to be inspected and accepted at our works by a representative of Lane Bros. Company with steam or without steam or both, and must be in thorough condition to satisfy their inspector, or they will have privilege to cancel order.*
>
> *Locomotive to be equipped with steam brake similar to your locomotive #36, either before shipment, or to be furnished to you after shipment and to be placed on locomotive by you, and the present hand brake shipped back to us. Front and Back Coupler to be similar to your #36 locomotive, and to be furnished in the same manner as the brake if necessary.*
>
> *Locomotive to be lettered, Lane Bros. Co., on both sides of tank, and number 39 on both sides of cab, and on front end.*

completed in 1910, and the records contain no further reference to the locomotive until 1914 when it was resold for the first time, and then again in 1918 when it was resold again to Lake Shore Sand & Gravel, a quarry operation on the shores of Lake Erie.

BRASS GONE

An interesting letter dated March 5, 1918 reveals that the locomotive was victimized by either a brass thief or an overzealous early railfan because all the brass disappeared from the locomotive while it was enroute to North East, Pennsylvania. The letter requesting replacement parts has prices written in, giving costs of locomotive brass in 1918. The last record of the locomotive was in 1927 when Lake Shore ordered a replacement cylinder head. This order and its handling are examples of the detailed Glover files. In 1927, a customer in extreme northern Pennsylvania mailed a parts order to Georgia on June 10. It was received and shipped three days later on June 13.

A colorful customer of the Glovers was the Due West Railway Company, Due West, South Carolina. This was one of the few Glover customers to use Glover locomotives in main line or common carrier service. Locomotive #12162 was shipped via the Southern Railway to its interchange with the Due West Railway at Donalds, South Carolina on April 9, 1910. Due West's President, R.S. Galloway, also was a principal in the Associate Reformed Presbyterian Church. Legend has it that the strict doctrine of this church dictated that the Due West, while engaged in common carrier service, never carried whiskey, and never carried anything on Sunday. In 1940, Frank Ardrey, Jr. photographed the #12162 at Donalds after the Due West ceased operations, and no further information on this locomotive has been found.

QUICK TURNAROUND

Locomotive #121619 was outshopped on July 14, 1913 and four days later at noon on July 18, the locomotive arrived back at the shop wrecked. Records do not reveal what happened, but the timing certainly indicates that the locomotive was damaged in transit to the customer. Records also state that less than 24 hours after the damaged locomotive arrived at the Glover shop, it was repaired and reshipped at 10:50 a.m. on July 19.

Old letterhead business stationary is often colorful, informative and quite fascinating. A wide selection was found in the files of locomotive #121623,

41

12162 as built 232

12162

> Glover Machine Works,
>   Marietta Ga.   *Due West, S.C.,*   *Sept 13*   **191** *1*
> Gentlemen,
>   *I wrote you some days ago about sending a man here to see about setting these valves. Have heard nothing. The present condition of the engine is liable to wreck it. The flues are leaking & Mr. Rowland says it is liable to blow up. We have been runing our first engine until two days ago when it required a little work. The last two days we have been runing your engine & it looks like going to pieces. The engine is not proving up satisfactorily. We have not run it more than one third of the time since we bought it. Have to rely more on our old engine. If you can send a man say so & if you can not say so & we will look elsewhere.*
>   *At any rate let us hear from you. Mr. Rowland Says that thae Cylinder head you last sent us is about quarter inch larger than the other one & that these rings suit badly.*
>   Yours truly,

but unfortunately, no builder's photo. Many of the successive owners of this locomotive used fancy stationary. The original owner was the Lodwick Lumber Company located in Shreveport, Louisiana, and the intended use of the engine is clearly depicted on Lodwick's stationary. The Woodward Wight Company assisted in shipping the locomotive, and their 1914 letterhead shows their company as being totally modernized with a fleet of motorized vehicles surrounding the premises, and not a horse in sight. Another Woodward Wight letterhead displays the incredible range of products and services offered. Some railroad letterheads are included as shipment of the locomotive is arranged. In 1925, a wagon company in Veach, Texas was in possession of #121623 and ordered parts for it on their letterhead. The last report on this locomotive was in 1926, when it was still in Texas.

121619   117

121619   274

The Lodwick Lumber Co., Inc.
S. B. HICKS, Pres.   J. T. WURTSBAUGH, V. Pres.   F. H. FORD, Sect & Treas.

MANUFACTURERS OF YELLOW PINE LUMBER

Shreveport, La.   1/21/1914.

Glover Machine Co.,
Marietta Ga.

Gentlemen:-

    We are going to need a locomotive for our Dyersdale Texas mill right soon and may possibly decide to buy a new machine rather than a second hand locomotive provided we could get prompt delivery, and will be galad to have you advise us your very best prices, and about what kind of delivery you can make. We rather think either engine listed in Catolog C under code words "Recod" and "Redon" might fill our requirements, possibly would want some slight changes. Also will be glad to have you send us specifications on K.& N.W. RR Engine #103, cut of which was left with us sometime ago; naming us lowest price on a duplicate of the locomotive.

    Trusting we may hear from you at an early date, and thanking you we beg to remain,

    Yours very truly,

JTW   THE LODWICK LUMBER CO.

WOODWARD, WIGHT & COMPANY
LIMITED
NEW ORLEANS, U.S.A.

April 30, 1914.
File "WAO"

Glover Machine Works,
Marietta, Ga.
Gentelmen:

    We are in receipt of a letter from the Lodwick Lumber Co., Inc, Shreveport, La. under date of April 28th, advising that you shipped a locomotive to us for their account. They do not give us the exact route over which this locomotive is traveling, and we would request that you kindly send us the original B/L, so we can take up with the proper railroad, and make the reconsignment on this shipment at once.

    We hope that you will mail us this B.L by return mail, so we can be on the lookout for this shipment.

    Thanking you for prompt attention, and awaiting to hear from you on this subject at an early date, we are in the meantime,

    Yours truly,

WAO-GBS

Chapter 6
The Biggest and the Fewest

The biggest cylinder locomotives built by the Glovers were 13 x 18", 14 x 20", 14 x 22", 15 x 20" and 16 x 20", and only 37 locomotives were built in these five cylinder sizes. Not even in these sizes were all of the locomotives built on standard gauge frames. Of the 37 units, 31 utilized the 13 x 18" and 14 x 20" cylinders, while only six locomotives were built with the three larger cylinders. Some Glover locomotive catalogs listed units being available with cylinders up to 17 x 20" and 18 x 24", but no records have been found to substantiate the building of these locomotives.

One of the best ways to gauge the success or failure of any product is to examine a company's records for repeat orders by their customers. Repeat orders exhibit a degree of satisfaction with a product, and in this regard the success of the locomotives built by the Glovers is proven: the Glovers enjoyed repeat orders from 10 of their customers.

114

735

PURCHASE FIVE LOCOS

One such customer was the Cherokee Brick Company in Macon, Georgia who, over the course of eight years, purchased five Glover locomotives. Two mid-sized locomotives were ordered by Cherokee Brick in 1912 and 1913, numbers #121610 and #121614. In June, 1916 an interesting letter was sent to the Glovers by a Mr. Dunwody of Cherokee Brick advising that they planned to tunnel under the Georgia Southern and Florida Railroad main line (now Norfolk Southern) to eliminate an at-grade crossing of the two railroads. The letterhead stationary is from Standard Brick Co. which, at that time, was a division of Cherokee Brick. Examination of the photographs of the earlier two locomotives, numbers #121610 and #121614, and the three subsequent locomotives, numbers #13186, #131810 and #131812 shows that something occurred to necessitate dropping of the cab, and Mr. Dunwody's letter gives the explanation.

It's also clear that they chose to purchase locomotives of slightly larger capacity by increasing the cylinder size. Once #13186 was on the property in late December, 1916, the high profile locomotives began to depart, with one leaving in 1917 and the other in 1918. The fate of #13186 is unknown, and the other two locomotives, #131810 and #131812 are believed to be the two recently donated to the Agrirama museum in Tifton, Georgia.

Locomotive #131811 was ordered in 1920 by the Anderson Lumber Corporation of Marion, South Carolina, and was shipped on Northern Pacific flat car #64469 on April 18 of that year. An undated letter from the customer appears in the file expressing the customer's complete satisfaction with the locomotive. Also in the file is a letter about a broken frame, representative of a common problem of that era. The technology of the time dictated the casting of large parts, and the casting process carried with it the danger of air pockets developing during pouring of metal into the mold.

CLIFFSIDE RAILROAD

A particularly interesting customer of the Glovers was the Cliffside Railroad at Cliffside, North Carolina. This company operated two Glover locomotives, #121626 purchased secondhand, and #131818 purchased new in 1923. On the cover sheet of the builder's file for #131818, its intended use was listed as "passenger service." This locomotive was still in service in 1940 when the last order for parts was processed.

```
                                COPY

Glover Machine Works,
Marietta, Ga.

Gentlemen:
         Referring to your letter of recent date, requesting
information regarding our # 3 Locomotive.
         First of all, our logging superintendent wishes me
to tell you, to put it in his exact language, "This engine
is the best damn engine Glover ever made!."

         He advises me that the---
            Average number of cars per trip is.......22
            Average number of feet per car is........3000
            Average length of haul.......... .........14 miles
            Worst grade..............................5 to 6%
         You understand these figures are not altogether
accurate, but are as near as could be estimated.
         Trust this information is what you desire.
                                Yours very truly,
CFA:W           Signed:   Anderson Lumber Corporation.
```

CABLE ADDRESS:-"ANDERSON"

ANDERSON LUMBER CORPORATION
MANUFACTURERS OF
PINE, CYPRESS AND HARDWOODS
GUM, RED, SAP AND TUPELO
ASH, MAPLE, OAK, POPLAR, PINE AND CYPRESS

MARION, S.C. Sept. 21, 1923.

> OFFICE OF
> # CLIFFSIDE RAILROAD COMPANY
>
> CLIFFSIDE, N. C. February 13, 1923.
>
> Mr. J. W. Glover,
> c/o Glover Machine Works,
> Marietta, Ga.
>
> Dear Sir:
>
> In order to have a record for our file, we confirm having bought from you to-day one of your 13x 18, six driver, double ender, side tank locomotives with back and front truck, complete automatic and straight air equipment, electric head lights back and front, for the sum of $10,750.00 f.o.b. your works. You to take as part payment either one or both (our option) of our numbers 1 and 5 Forney Type locomotives at $1,000.00 each f.o.b. here.
>
> It is understood that the locomotive you furnish us is guaranteed to meet the inspection of the Hartford Insurance Company, also to comply with all requirements of the Interstate Commerce Commission.
>
> According to agreement, we will expect you to make up specifications complete and send us for approval.
>
> Yours very truly,
> CLIFFSIDE RAILROAD COMPANY,
> Chas H Haynes
> President
>
> CHH/U

Smith valve gear 465

A colorful piece of the Glover's locomotive story began in 1919 when the company was engaged to build two locomotives for a customer in Russia. Locomotives #142011 and #142012 left Marietta in October, 1920 where they were to be loaded aboard the *S.S. Lordship Manor* at Philadelphia to sail for Europe. With Russia's prolonged use of steam power the continued existence of these engines has to be questioned.

J.W. Motley of New York crops up frequently in the Glover files, and he did so again in 1917 and 1918. This time he was involved in the sale of four locomotives to the Haitian American Sugar Co. (HASCO) of Port-au-Prince, Haiti. Over the course of a year, they purchased 30" gauge locomotives #142010, #15201, #15202 and #15203. The #142010 was a 2-6-0, while the 1520 series locomotives were all 2-6-2s. The 1520s were equipped with Vanderbilt-style tenders with rear-mounted apparatus for what must have been frequent or lengthy reverse moves. A second feature of the HASCO locomotives that sets them apart is their Smith valve gear, designed by W.L. Smith, master mechanic for HASCO. The files contain photographs of the gear, as well as instructions for setting and adjusting its operation.

Some of the HASCO files show the original purchase order for the first HASCO locomotive built, locomotive #142010, along with terms of sale for all four locomotives, and a letter from the subcontractor who built the Vanderbilt style tenders. The W&A bill of lading is included along with the contents list for each piece count showing what an enormous task the customer was faced with when his new locomotive arrived in kit form.

Another document reveals the pressure applied to speed delivery time of the customer's three 15 x 20" locomotives by calling on the U.S. government. The main reason for production delays during 1917 and 1918 was the lack of availability of material due to America's declaration of war in April, 1917. This development is underscored by a letter with its War stamp affixed from one of the Glover's suppliers. Parts were still being ordered for these locomotives well into the 1940s, and new boilers for all were priced in 1940 at $2,400 each, and other parts ordered until 1948.

LARGEST LOCOMOTIVE

The largest locomotive the Glovers built, as part of a two unit order, was a 16 x 20" locomotive built for the Graves Lumber Co. located in Hosford, Florida.

The other locomotive was #12165, and the #16201 was just that, the first and last of that size. Gearing the foundry to cast cylinders for a single locomotive probably made the #16201 an expensive project for the Glovers, as well as for the customer. The price of this locomotive was $11,800, compared to a 12 x 16" locomotive selling in the $4,000-$5,000 range.

Shipping a locomotive of this size presented different circumstances for the Glovers as indicated on the NC&StL bill of lading showing the locomotive shipped "under steam," and in the W&A response to the Glover's request to sell them markers and flags to meet requirements for shipment of the locomotive. Parts for the locomotive were ordered by the original customer until 1927, but there the story ends, and we're left to wonder what became of this, the biggest Glover locomotive.

While the last Glover locomotive didn't leave the shop until 1930, by the 1920s some subtle hints began to appear that steam was beginning to experience competition. Electric motors and internal combustion had become mature sources of power for many applications that a decade or two before would have been dominated by steam. In many respects, this transformation was completed a decade or two later when the diesel locomotive finished the job.

CAN'T LOCATE BOILERS

A set of letters found in the files of locomotive #7128, some on artistic letterhead stationary, reflect the changing demand for steam power. By 1926 the Glovers encountered unaccustomed difficulty in locating a boiler shop to produce the relatively small boiler for a 7 x 12" cylinder locomotive. By this time, internal combustion or electricity was the power of choice for machinery of this size, and for one reason or another, of the 11 companies contacted, seven shops turned the Glover orders down.

The Glover locomotive construction era ended in 1930, with the continued production of locomotive parts continuing well into the 1940s. The last piece of correspondence found that puts an end to this chapter in the Glover story is a letter dated May 13, 1946 when the Glovers declined an offer from J.M. Motley to bid on an order for 25 locomotives.

By this time, the majority of the Glover facility and resources were devoted to their highly successful production and marketing of high pressure pipeline fittings, and the enormous interference in that area by the production of steam-powered equipment or parts could no longer be tolerated.

UNITED STATES FOOD ADMINISTRATION
WASHINGTON, D. C.
November 6, 1917.

IN YOUR REPLY REFER TO
H-31-D

Glover Machine Works,
    Marietta, Ga.
Gentlemen:

The Haytian American Corporation calls to the attention of the Sugar Department, Food Administration, certain order for locomotives placed with your company. In view of the sugar shortage and the fact that this company will be in position to grind 200,000 tons of cane in February, 1918, if various items of material are delivered on time, it is our hope that you will make an effort so to do. We have no disposition to request priority certificates, much preferring to leave the matter in your own hands. In due course will you kindly advise prospects.

Yours truly,
U. S. FOOD ADMINISTRATION.
By Edward Chambers

Dec. 12, 1910.

Mr. J. A. Baldwin, Ass't. Sup't.,
    W. & A. R. R.,
        Atlanta, Ga.

Dear Sir,—

We have a Locomotive that we expect to ship in about ten days under its own steam to Hosfords, Fla., on the Apalatchicola, Northern Railroad. In order to send this engine out it will be necessary for us to have a complete set of markers for both front and rear, and also a complete set of flags. We have not time to get these from the factory in the North, and would appreciate very much if you would sell same to us, and if you can do so please have same delivered to us through your Agent at Marietta between now and the 20th.

Awaiting your advices, we are,
    Yours truly,
        GLOVER MACHINE WORKS.

16201 102

Chapter 7
Photo Gallery

A gallery of photos were taken by the Glover family over a period from 1902, when locomotive #8141 was recorded for history before being shipped on May 6 of that year, until December of 1924 when locomotive #10169 was documented.

Glover photography was an "in-house" proposition performed by the Glover family. The result is an informal, entertaining group of photographs, in contrast to other formal builder's photographs. Look carefully at the "clutter" in many of the photos and see how many locomotive parts can be identified. Look for workmen peeking around the photo backdrop. And look for J.B. Glover's shadow in the foreground of some of the photos as he bends under a black cloth to focus his camera and record the view. Because so many Glover locomotives were built to narrow gauge specifications, they were delivered to customers on flat cars and they are interesting themselves.

Each photo has been identified by a glass plate number and by the builder's number. For more information on a specific locomotive, refer to the locomotive roster at the back of the book where each locomotive is listed in builder's number sequence.

Littlest

581   574

581   655

7126   335

7125   17

7127   790

8141   385

8144   384

8146   388   7124   348

81417   373

81424   697

Child in photograph is James Bolan Glover, III.

81418   29

91410   37   9141   368

9142   328

9149 445

91414 66

91415 68

91416 665

Brookside No. 2

Light Six Wheel Connected Saddle Tank Locomotive

		Nag	Nail	Nap
Code Word				
Cylinders { Diameter, inches		7	8	9
Cylinders { Stroke, inches		12	14	14
Diameter of Driving Wheels, inches		24	24	24
Rigid Wheel Base, feet and inches		5–6	5–6	5–6
Length over all, feet and inches		14–0	14–6	14–9
Extreme height above rail, feet and inches		8–6	9–0	9–0
Weight of Engine in working order, pounds		20000	25000	30000
Water capacity of tank, gallons		300	400	500
Fuel capacity { Coal, pounds		250	250	300
Fuel capacity { Wood, cubic feet		20	20	25
Weight per yard of lightest rail, advisable, pounds		20	20	25
Radius of sharpest curve, practicable, feet		35	35	40
Radius of sharpest curve, advisable, feet		55	55	55
Boiler pressure, per square inch, pounds		160	160	160
Tractive force, pounds		3320	5070	6020
Hauling Capacity in Tons of 2000 Pounds (Exclusive of Locomotive)				
On absolute level		503	769	928
On ½ per cent grade—6 inch to 100 feet		202	296	352
On 1 " " —1 foot to 100 feet		118	176	214
On 2 " " —2 feet to 100 feet		63	95	112
On 3 " " —3 feet to 100 feet		43	60	65

H. S. SHANER
PRESIDENT, GENERAL MANAGER
AND PURCHASING AGENT

A.L. HALE
VICE PRESIDENT AND TREASURER

W.E. THOMAS
SECOND VICE PRESIDENT AND SECRETARY

H.C. SHANER
GENERAL SUPERINTENDENT AND
SUPERINTENDENT OF EQUIPMENT

ST. LOUIS, LITTLE ROCK AND GULF RAILROAD CO.

CAPITAL STOCK, $4,000,000.00

LITTLE ROCK, ARK. April 26 1904

Mr. W. F. Davis,
   Birmingham, Ala.

Dear Sir;

Yours of 4/25-04 to hand.   and in reply will say, as yet we have not ordered   any engines, but will ask you to quote your best prices on, two 17 by 24, 4 wheel connected passenger engines, to have a general over-hauling, and your best terms on same, on payments, and oblige,

Yours,
President. H.S. Shaner

523 1/2 Main St.

Middleweights

10141 as rebuilt   49

10141 as built   391

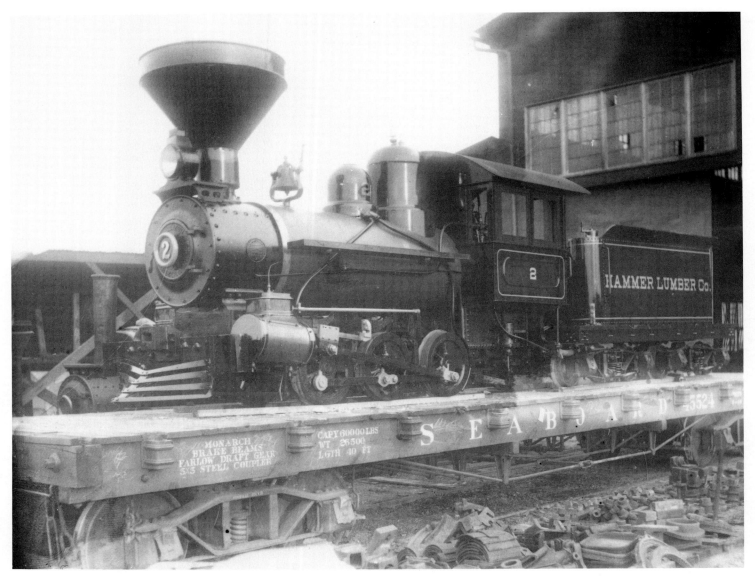

10146 374

10147 73

Child on ground is James Bolan Glover, III. Man in cab window is George Welsh, mechanical engineer with Glover Machine Works.

10149   124

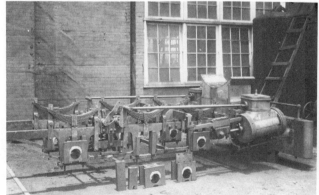

101410   154

101413   129

101419   417   101418   186

101426 & 27   349

101425   346

101428   547

63

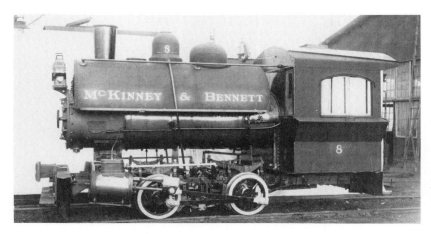

101430   527

101438   860

101431   544

101433   604

101434   598

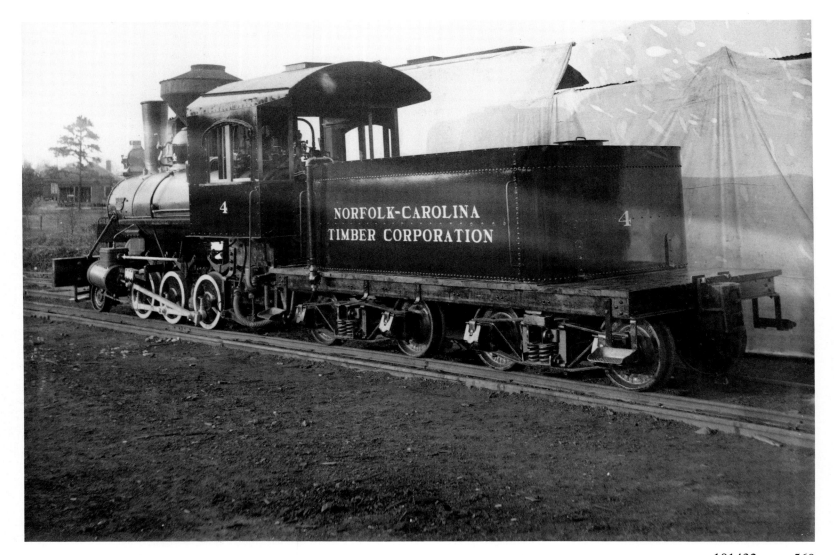

101432   569

101432   570

L to R #10161 #10162 #? 365   10161 or 10162   387

67

10165 69

10166 136

10167

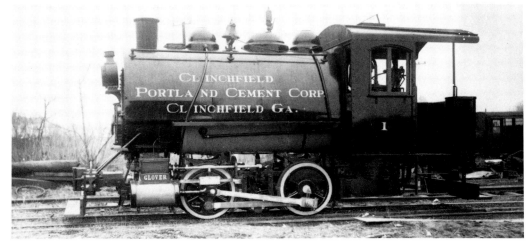

10169

11163 41

11163 610

12161   233

12163   228

12165   218   12165   205

12165   214

A view of #12166 in 1911 built for its original owner, Mayo Lumber. 12166   59

In 1919, #12166 was ready for its third owner, Twin Tree. 12166   738

12167   220

121620   187

12169   222

121621   60

This was #121610 in 1910 lettered for its original owner, Cherokee Brick.   121610   65

121610   736   With saddletank removed and new tender lettered for Tuxbury, this was #121610 in 1920.

121622   181

121624   176

121627   543

121629   576

77

121629 561

121629 580

121630 444A

121631   498

121631   505A

121632 323

121633 619

121634   669

121636   700B

121635   701

81

121637   677

121639   789

121639   229

121641   884   121640   820

83

121642   876

In February 1972, #121645 was photographed on Route 30 on its way from Caguas to Juncos, Puerto Rico.

Biggest

13181 226

13181 238

13181 242

13181 236

13186   538   13183   188

13188 751   13187 564

87

13188 & 13189   754

13188   793

13188   791

13189   709

13189   783

131810   733

131810   733B

131813   802

131816   765

131816   766

131817   822

131818   869

14201 366

14202 31

Pictured from left to right are Aimee Dunwody Glover, Mrs. A. S. J. Gardner, Mrs. John Wilder Glover and James Bolan Glover, III.

14203   97

14207   357

14209   589   14208   513

98

This was one of two units shipped to Russia. Its tender was lettered "Communist."

This was the second unit shipped to Russia; the tender was lettered "Internationalist."

142012

142013   660

100

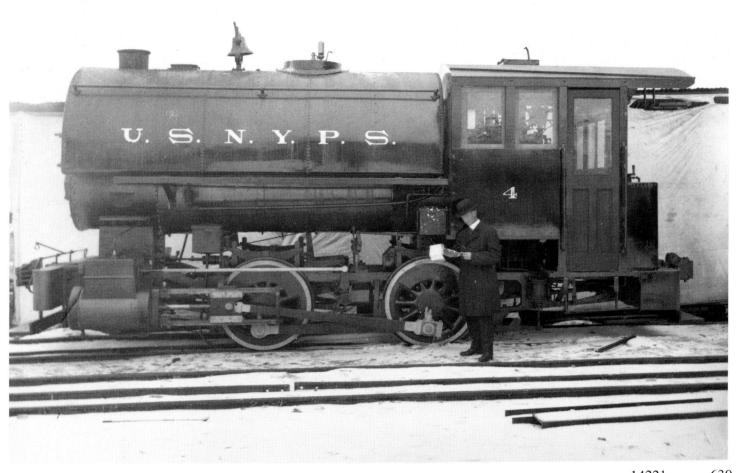

15201   745

14221   630

15203 858

15203 864

15204 673

102

Chapter 8
Puzzle Pages

The Glover records present many puzzles that can be frustrating because of a lack of information, but at the same time fun and rewarding when pieces of information come together to solve another part of the puzzle. With the flexibility of a relatively small shop, informal recordkeeping with attendant gaps in information, locomotives coming and going as trade-ins and rebuilds, lots of questions still need answers and clarification.

Here are some puzzles, and some of the fun and frustration that go along with them.

Plate #54   There isn't any information on this locomotive. It looks like a Glover, but it cannot be identified.

Plate #171   This looks like a Glover with its round builder's plate and curved cab window top, but no written record of the St. John's Lumber Co. was found.

Plate #376   No records for L.D. Yancy. Locomotive on the right is #9142.

Plate #379   The lady occupying the fireman's seat is unknown; no identification for the locomotives.

Plates #394, 399, 422 and 429 (399 and 422 shown) This is a particularly interesting puzzle. These four photos are captioned in the archives as "Stratton Brick Yard, Macon, Georgia." In 1903, Stratton Brick Co. became Cherokee Brick Co. Refer in the Photo Gallery (page 49) to Glover engine #8141, plate #385, also attributed to the Stratton Brick Company. This locomotive is similar but there are profound differences.

Plate #433   Is this a trade-in? The two children are James Bolan Glover, III and Aimee Dunwody Glover, brother and sister.

Plate #437   What a gorgeous old 2-6-0 with its ornate steam and sand domes. Note the locomotive amidst so much clutter. No record was found of the W.L. Robinson Lumber Company, and this does not look like a Glover-built engine. Was it a trade-in, or just in for repairs?

Plate #438 This odd-looking machine was a trade-in from the Etna Steel and Iron Company of Etna, Georgia. No other information was given.

Plate # 448   This may be the longest 0-4-0 ever seen (both in overall length and wheel base)—and probably the ugliest. Who made it?

Plate #450 Another mystery and another fine photograph. The builder's plate in the foreground looks like #121822, but no records of a locomotive such as this were found with that cylinder size. Is this another unknown engine to add to the Glover total?

Plate #622 What a great way to be able to fully appreciate the tremendous difference in size between some of the Glover products! The locomotive in the background is #14221, but there is no identification on the little critter in the foreground. It was destined for a life overseas because it has one of Mr. Motley's brass tags on the side of the cab below the window.

Plates #427 and 430 Both photos carry the name *J. P. Boyle* in the Glover's files. Photo 430 shows the builder's plate; the number on it appears to be #7122. Engine #7122 was, in fact, sold to J. P. Boyle. The records show that several years after its original sale the locomotive was returned as a trade-in. Might photo #427 be the same locomotive after rebuilding?

Epilogue

Often, when an in-depth study is made of a particular subject, the results must be categorized as a "work in progress." That is the case with this on-going study.

It would take years of full time work to review all of the records in the Glover archives. Many questions remain unanswered, not the least of which is the number of locomotives the Glovers built. Less than 200 are documented, but it seems certain more were constructed.

JUST BEGINNING

We have provided information on how far-flung the distribution of Glover locomotives was via the used locomotive market, based on Glover records. Other records exist, such as research done by Tom Lawson in Birmingham, Alabama, that expand on the Glover's records. So far, we have not uncovered information relating to the many locomotives the Glovers took in trade. And where are the missing 78 glass plate negatives, and what treasures might they contain? There is much yet to be learned, much new information to be gathered, and maybe this is just the beginning.

For a model railroader, there is nothing quite as frustrating as having a completed model railroad, because building it is 90% of the fun. And so it is with this project. Building the complete story is fun, and it's a project with plenty of life left.

COMPANY MOVES

As this book is being completed, the Glover complex in Marietta has been sold, and the company will consolidate its operations in a newer facility in Cordele, Georgia. A serious attempt is under way to establish a facility to receive all of the historical holdings of the Glover family. The vision is that an archives will enable research by serious students of history, that the hardwood patterns will be cleaned and inventoried so that the casting of locomotive parts can be done utilizing turn-of-the-century casting methods, and that the two locomotives on the property will be restored to operating condition.

The vision is that the Glover locomotive story not end with the sale of the property where they were built, because the Glover locomotive story is too important to the history of the industrialization of the South. Previous generations of the Glover family and the current generation have done an incredible job of safeguarding their history. Honoring what they have done to preserve this important part of the history of the South is now up to our generation.

The "last" complete Glover locomotive, an 0-4-0, is removed by crane from the Marietta plant in fall of 1995. It sat in one end of the foundry after being returned for non-payment of the invoice.

Dick Hillman

Locomotive Roster

This locomotive roster was produced from Glover records. Other records exist as to owners of Glover locomotives, but the decision was made to include only the history as told in these archives. The name appearing next to the builder's number is the original purchaser of each locomotive, with subsequent owners, if any, appearing in sequence below.

It became something of a quandary to determine dates for the production of a given locomotive. There is the date the locomotive was ordered, the date that the work began, the date the boiler was inspected and the date the locomotive was shipped.

For purposes of consistency, the most frequently found date in the records, and a date that seems the most accurate, was the date from the bill of lading that showed when the locomotive was shipped from the Glover Works. In most cases, the letter "S" appears next to the date, meaning the date the locomotive was shipped. In cases where a bill of lading was not found, the letter "O" appears, meaning the date the locomotive was ordered. If a zero appears in a date (i.e. 5-0-28), it means that no day of the month was found in the records.

BUILDER'S NUMBER	OWNER(S) & ROAD NUMBER	ORIG. OWNER	SUBSEQ. OWNERS	DATE S = SHIPPED O = ORDERED	GAUGE & TYPE	REMARKS	GLASS PLATE #
581	U.S. Naval Coal Depot #1 San Diego	CA		3-21-17 S	24" 0-4-0T		573, 574, 587, 655
582	U.S. Naval Coal Depot #2 San Diego	CA		3-21-17 S	24" 0-4-0T		573, 587, 725
583	(Owner Unknown) South Africa	*		2-16-18 S	36" 0-4-0T	J.M. Motley & C.H. McCarthy, N.Y. City both brokered sale	
584	United Fruit Co. Santa Maria, Columbia	*		12-0-22 S	36" 0-4-0T	Lettered "Eusebia." Used on banana plantation	861, 863
7121	Excelsior Coal Excelsior	KY		4-30-04 S	42" 0-4-0T		383
	Addington, F.A. Lanvale		SC	5-0-20			
7122	Boyle, J.P. Williams Landing	NC		10-11-05 S	36" 0-4-2F	Returned & rebuilt January, 1908. Taken in as part payment for #81415. Boyle #2	427, 430
7123	Terault, Jos. Cresswell	NC		5-22-05 S	36" 0-4-2F	Terault became Pittsburg Land & Lumber, 1909	55
	Wisconsin Lumber Co. Cresswell		NC	8-15-13		Wisconsin Lumber in financial trouble 1914. Unit may have reverted to Pittsburg Land & Lumber	
	Vineland Lumber Co. Vineland		NC	0-0-20			
	Goose Creek Lumber Co. Charleston		SC	1-30-26			
7124	Sloss Sheffield Steel & Iron #3 Flat Top	AL		8-27-06 S	Std. 0-4-0T	Unit rented to Swansboro Land & Lumber 9-4-13	279, 348
7125	Tennessee Coal, Iron & RR Co. #17 Blossburg	AL		6-29-10 S	36" 0-6-0T		16, 17

BUILDER'S NUMBER	OWNER(S) & ROAD NUMBER	ORIG. OWNER	SUBSEQ. OWNERS	DATE S = SHIPPED O = ORDERED	GAUGE & TYPE	REMARKS	GLASS PLATE #
7126	Mutual Mining Co. #2 Dutton	FL		4-12-11 S	36" 0-4-0T		19, 335
	McCoy Brick & Tile Augusta		GA	6-0-19			
	McShan J.T. Lumber McShan		AL	11-0-19			
7127	Samana & Santiago Ry #3 Sanchez, Dominican Republic	•		9-25-19 S	42" 0-4-2F	Unit never exported, probably returned to Glovers	704, 707, 710, 727, 744
	Reynolds Coal Co. Grafton		WV	2-0-26			
7128	Splint Jellico Coal Co. #2 Lafollette	TN		6-30-26 S	40" 0-4-0T	Used 3 months only, repossessed by Glovers Dec. 1927. Still in shop, 1995	
8141	Stratton Brick Co. Macon	GA		5-6-02 S	36" 0-4-0T	Appears to be 1st locomotive built. Builders sheets are only records. In 1903, Stratton became Cherokee	385
8142	Trimble Brick Co. Hogansville	GA		3-14-03 S	36" 0-4-0T		
	Southern Clay Co. Sumter		SC	9-0-16		Unit at James Crossing, SC. Southern Clay became Interstate Clay, March 1917.	
	Georgia Kaolin Co. Dry Branch		GA	4-26-19			
8143	Elk Valley Coal & Coke Elk Valley	TN		6-17-03 S	40" 0-4-0		
	Splint Jellico Coal Elk Valley		TN	1-26-22			
8144	Campbell Coal & Coke Orme	TN		9-14-03 S	36" 0-4-0T		384
8145	Rome Brick Co. Rome	GA		5-3-04 S	36" 0-4-0T		445
	Griffin Press Brick Co. Griffin		GA	6-25-10			
8146	Alabama Virginia Iron Co. #1 Russellville	AL		9-17-04 S	36" 0-4-0T	Lettered "the Douglas"	388, 390
	Pinkney Mining Co. Russelville		AL	3-16-17			
8147	Alabama Construction Co. Cartersville	GA		1-0-05 S	36" 0-4-0T	Lettered "Lacy". Returned to Glovers for rebuilding Jan. 1913	
	Jacksonboro Lumber Co. Charleston		SC	1-0-13		Rebuild included steel cab	
8148	Alabama Construction Co. Cartersville	GA		0-0-0	36" 0-4-0T	Lettered "Walton"	370
	South Carolina Clay Co. #2 Langley		SC	3-17-13			
	McNamee Kaolin Co. Bath		SC	0-0-24			
8149	Alabama & Georgia Iron Co. Cedartown	GA		4-20-05 O	36" 0-4-0T		

BUILDER'S NUMBER	OWNER(S) & ROAD NUMBER	ORIG. OWNER	SUBSEQ. OWNERS	DATE S = SHIPPED O = ORDERED	GAUGE & TYPE	REMARKS	GLASS PLATE #
	Richardson Mining Co. Cedartown		GA	0-0-14			
81410	Chattahoochee Brick Co. #1 Atlanta	GA		5-15-06 S	36" 0-4-0T		
81411	Avent, R.C. #4 Moss Point	MS		6-0-06 S	Std. 0-6-4F	Returned Jan. 1908 & rebuilt as 10143	56, 360
	Munger & Bennett #6 New Bern		NC	3-16-08		Now Glover #10143	
81412	Chattanooga Iron & Coal Dunlap	TN		10-24-06 S	36" 0-4-0T		371
81413	Atlanta Mining & Clay Co. Atlanta	GA		1-1-07 S	36" 0-4-0T	Unit at Gresham, GA	
	Georgia Kaolin Co. Dry Branch		GA	1-0-20			
81414	Grace, J.W. Puerto Cortez, Honduras	•		2-8-07 S	Std. 0-6-4F	Customer's name: Cuyamel Fruit Co.	
81415	Boyle, J.P. #2 Hamilton	NC		10-1-07 S	36" 0-4-0		140, 418
	Farmer's Mfg. Co. Norfolk		VA	3-1-15		Unit at Lewiston, NC	
81416	Blades, J.B. Lumber Co. #1 New Bern	NC		11-5-07 S	Std. 0-4-0	Unit at Newport, NC	57
81417	Campbell Coal Mining #1 Westbourne	TN		11-20-07 S	36" 0-4-0T	Returned for rebuilding, 1922	373
	Pratt Consolidated Coal Co. Gamble Mine		AL	7-13-22			
	Alabama Byproducts Corp. Tarrant		AL	2-0-26			
81418	Cook Jellico Coal Co. #1 Jellico	TN		6-27-12 S	36" 0-4-0T	Dropped Cab. Customer defaulted 1916, unit returned 1918. Delay in return of 2 yrs. due to miner's strike.	27, 28, 382
81419	Jacksonville Lumber Co. #1 Jacksonville	NC		10-19-12 S	36" 0-4-2F	Not a new locomotive. #91410 returned by 2nd owner Sept. 1911 & rebuilt into 81419.	67
81420	Reed, J. Davis #1 Portsmouth	VA		4-8-14 S	Std. 0-4-4F		178, 189
	Williamston Cooperage Co. Williamston		NC	5-0-17			
81421	Coulbourne Bros. #4 Suffolk	VA		1-0-17 S	36" 2-6-0	Returned for repair/resale in 1923, never sold.	540, 542, 545
81422	Dupont Engineering #6 Hermitage	TN		4-18-18 S	36" 0-4-0T	Used in United States Ordnance Facility	672A, 672B, 695
	Muncey Coal Mining Co. Krypton		KY	2-16-22			
81423	Dupont Engineering #7 Hermitage	TN		5-18-18 S	36" 0-4-0T		696, 698
	Dempster Construction Co. Knoxville		TN	3-0-23		Used at St. Charles, KY & Swannannoa, NC 1925	

BUILDER'S NUMBER	OWNER(S) & ROAD NUMBER	ORIG. OWNER	SUBSEQ. OWNERS	DATE S = SHIPPED O = ORDERED	GAUGE & TYPE	REMARKS	GLASS PLATE #
81424	Dupont Engineering #8 Hermitage	TN		6-15-18 S	36" 0-4-0T		697
9141	Cotter, W.T. Jascksonville	FL		3-24-05 O	36" 0-4-0T		368
	Carolina Sand & Gravel Co. Carthage		NC	0-0-23			
9142	Gaffney Lime Co. #2 Gaffney	SC		1-0-06 S	Std. 0-4-0T	Parent Co.: Limestone Springs Lime Works	328
	Lehman, Chas. T. Birmingham		Al	3-17-16			
9143	Skinner, O.B. Compfield	SC		2-22-07 S	Std. 0-4-0T		
	Winyah Lumber Co. Georgetown		SC	4-12-13			
	Lachicotte, P.R. & Sons Waverly Mills		SC	4-20-18			
9144	Rome Furnace Co. Rome	GA		10-6-06 S	36" 0-4-0T	Unit at Cedartown, GA	
9145	Chattahoochee Brick Co. #3 Chattachoochee	GA		5-13-07 S	36" 0-4-0T		
9146	Etna Steel & Iron Etna	GA		4-25-07 S	36" 0-4-0T		
	Page Mining Co. Cartersville		GA	1-1-31			
9147	Squire, A.T. #4 Omega	FL		6-20-07 S	36" 0-6-2F		
9148	Palmer Brick Co. #2 Atlanta	GA		7-19-08 S	36" 0-4-0T		
	Chattahoochee Brick Co. Chattachoochee		GA	7-11-14			
9149	Rome Brick Co. #2 Rome	GA		5-10-10 S	36" 0-4-0T	Lettered "Florence-Emily"	445
	Edgar Bros Co. McIntyre		GA	4-0-23			
	Chattahoochee Brick Co. Chattachoochee		GA	2-24-25			
91410	Kessler & Dehone #2 Kessler	LA		9-0-10	36" 0-4-2F	Unit returned 1-24-11	37, 51
	Baum & Van Roy #2 Crystal River		FL	2-24-11		Unit returned 9-8-11 & rebuilt as #81419	
91411	Clark Lumber Co. #5 Jacksonville	FL		11-28-10 S	36" 0-4-0T	Unit at Palatka, FL. Customer defaulted July, 1912 & unit repossessed.	
	Trimble Brick Co. #2 Trimble		GA	7-31-13			
91412	Russellville Iron Ore & Mining #3 Russellville	AL		5-24-10 S	36" 0-4-0T		

BUILDER'S NUMBER	OWNER(S) & ROAD NUMBER	ORIG. OWNER	SUBSEQ. OWNERS	DATE S = SHIPPED O = ORDERED	GAUGE & TYPE	REMARKS	GLASS PLATE #
	Alabama Fuel & Iron Co. Birmingham		AL	6-16-10		Alabama Fuel & Iron purchased Russellville, operated under name I.C. Delony	
91413	Same as 91412 #4				36" 0-4-0T		
91414	Wade, J.T. #1 Savannah	GA		11-15-11 S	Std. 0-6-0T		26, 66
91415	McRainey & Bridges #1 Wildwood	FL		7-13-12 S	Std. 0-4-0		68, 72
	Holsema, J.C. Mfg. Co. Jacksonville	.	FL	12-1-19			
91416	Sloss Sheffield Steel & Iron #3 Dora	AL		7-7-17 S	Std. 0-4-0T		665
91417	Sloss Sheffield Steel & Iron #2 Brookside	AL		5-3-17 O	Std. 0-6-0T		594, 618
91418	Ladson Brick & Tile Co. #1 Moultrie	GA		4-9-21 S	36" 0-4-0T	Unit at Kingwood, GA. Company out of business 1924. No disposition of locomotive	819, 828, 829
91419	(Never Sold)			0-0-0	36" 0-4-0T	Unfinished unit never sold. Still in shop, 1995.	
10141	Swansboro Land & Lumber Co. Swansboro	NC		3-23-07 S	Std. 2-6-0	Unit returned 10-12-08. Rebuilt with cylinders relocated 12" further forward.	49, 132, 372, 391
	Munger & Bennett #2 New Bern		NC	12-22-19			
	Mizelle, J.I. Logging Newport		NC	3-15-24			
10142	Tennessee Coal, Iron & RR Co. Smythe	AL		6-7-07 S	36" 0-4-0T		
10143	Munger & Bennett Lumber #6 New Bern	NC		3-16-08 S	Std. 0-6-0	Originally built as 81411	126, 141
	Mizelle, J.I. Logging Newport		NC	11-12-20			
10144	Neal Naval Stores #1 Jacksonville	FL		7-13-11 S	Std. 0-4-4F		38, 50, 52
	Boyd, E.M. Co. Crescent City		FL	8-5-12			
	S&A Lumber Co. Hastings		FL	8-13-15			
	Roy Lumber Co. Jennings		FL	5-23-18			
	Wilson-Otwell & Cone Lebanon		FL	12-10-23		Company operated Crystal River Crate	
10145	Suffolk Lumber Co. #1 Jacksonville	NC		6-8-11 S	36" 0-4-4F		61, 64
	Onslow Lumber Co. Jacksonville		NC	2-24-13			
	Rankin, Chas. Lumber Hallsboro		NC	4-13-17			

BUILDER'S NUMBER	OWNER(S) & ROAD NUMBER	ORIG. OWNER	SUBSEQ. OWNERS	DATE S = SHIPPED O = ORDERED	GAUGE & TYPE	REMARKS	GLASS PLATE #
10146	Hammer Lumber Co. #2 New Bern	NC		3-7-10 S	36" 0-6-0	Returned & rebuilt, June 1920	121, 374
	Beaufort County Lumber Co. Fairmont		NC	1-18-22			
10147	Kessler & Dehone #2 Belle Rose	LA		10-30-10 S	36" 0-4-2F	Lettered "Marion". 10147 replaces 91410 deemed too small & returned.	73, 74, 334
	Lula Co. Belle Rose		LA	7-25-18			
10148	Walterboro Lumber Co. #1 Walterboro	SC		3-18-11 S	Std. 2-6-0		118, 125, 138, 244
	Osceola Cypress Co. Bridgne		FL	8-12-21			
10149	Anderson, L. & Co. Timmonsville	SC		2-23-11 S	Std. 0-6-0		124, 135
	Myakka Lumber Co. Arcadia		FL	6-20-22			
101410	Baum & Van Roy Crate Co. #2 Crystal River	FL		8-19-11 S	36" 0-6-0	Baum & Van Roy become Crystal River Crate, Nov. 1920	123, 133
	Leavy County Timber Co. Lennon		FL	8-0-24			
101411	Enville Lumber Co. #10 Enville	FL		4-16-12 S	Std. 0-6-0		441
	Hart Lumber Co. Brooksville		FL	2-27-13			
	Denton Lumber Co. Centralia		FL	4-15-14			
	Fox J.P. Lumber Co. Balm		FL	3-2-17			
	Sweat Lumber Co Mizpah		FL	10-30-24			
101412	Levert Lumber & Shingle Co. #1 Placquemine	LA		1-19-12 S	Std. 0-6-0		217
	Atchafalya Timber Co. Elliott City		LA	5-28-14			
	Cameron Lumber Co. Smoaks		SC	12-13-20			
	McNeill, H.J. Springfield		SC	11-6-26			
101413	Brinson, B.F. #2 Lake City	FL		10-9-12 S	Std. 0-6-0		129, 185
	Yellow Pine Operating Co. Maytown		FL	8-31-18			
	Union Cypress Co. Hopkins		FL	5-9-21			
	Standard Lumber Co. Egypt		GA	11-28-24			

BUILDER'S NUMBER	OWNER(S) & ROAD NUMBER	ORIG. OWNER	SUBSEQ. OWNERS	DATE S = SHIPPED O = ORDERED	GAUGE & TYPE	REMARKS	GLASS PLATE #
101414	Lacy, C.W. #20 Nashville	TN		12-0-12 S	36" 0-4-0T		
101415	Lacy, C.W. #21 Nashville	TN		12-0-12 S	36" 0-4-0T		115
	Monday, M.C. E. Chattanooga		TN	12-1-19			
101416	Chatham Lumber Co. #3 (no location given)			0-0-0	Std. 0-6-0		131, 134
	Tyson, S.W. #1 Leary		GA	9-12-13			127
	Garbutt, R.M. #1 Savannah		GA	0-0-0			
101417	Sloss Sheffield Steel & Iron #1 Brookside	AL		9-4-13	Std. 0-4-0T		63
101418	Little River Lumber Co. #2 Princeton	NC		11-10-13 S	36" 0-4-0		58, 120, 186, 240
	Hammer Lumber Co. Wilmington		NC	12-1-19		Unit at Little River, SC	
	Beaufort County Lumber Co. Fairmont		NC	1-18-22		Unit at Little River, SC	
	Pate, Charles T. Conway		SC	1-1-25			
	West, M.M. & Co. Conway		SC	2-24-26			
101419	Roanoke River Log Co. #3 Lewiston	NC		12-6-13 S	36" 2-6-0		119, 184, 417
	Farmers Mfg. Co. Lewiston		NC	3-1-15			
	North State Lumber Co. Charleston		SC	0-0-0			
101420	Mungter & Bennett #8 New Bern	NC		3-19-14 S	36" 2-6-0		183
	Adams, S.H. Cooperage New Bern		NC	1-20-20			
	Eubank W.M. Lumber Scotts Hill		NC	8-7-26			
101421	Small, A. T. Quarries Macon	GA		5-12-14 S	Std. 0-4-0T		770
	Morris Stone Co. Holton		GA	9-23-25			
	Macon Crushed Granite Co. Holton		GA	11-19-26			
101422	Appomattox Box Shook Co. #1 Petersburgh	VA		5-2-16 S	Std. 2-6-0		324, 326
	Maco Lumber Co. Maco		NC	12-20-27		Loco offered for sale to Glovers by Maco Lumber 12-20-27	

BUILDER'S NUMBER	OWNER(S) & ROAD NUMBER	ORIG. OWNER	SUBSEQ. OWNERS	DATE S = SHIPPED O = ORDERED	GAUGE & TYPE	REMARKS	GLASS PLATE #
	Beech Island Lumber Co. Stedman		NC	5-21-28			
	Greene Bros. Lumber Co. Stedman		NC	8-9-33			
101423	Sloss Sheffield Steel & Iron #26 Russellville	AL		11-13-15 S	36" 0-4-0T		343, 345, 351
101424	Sloss Sheffield Steel & Iron #10 Russellville	AL		9-15-15 S	Std. 0-4-0T	Lettered "Ivy"	
101425	Sloss Sheffield Steel & Iron #27 Russellville	AL		11-13-15 S	36" 0-4-0T		346, 351
101426	Sloss Sheffield Steel & Iron #28 Russellville	AL		1-1-16 S	36" 0-4-0T		349, 352
101427	Sloss Sheffield Steel & Iron #29 Russellville	AL		1-1-16 S	36" 0-4-0T		349, 350
101428	Zickgraf Lumber Co. #4 Arcola	FL		1-29-17 S	Std. 0-6-0		547, 548
101429	Garris, C.W. #1 Groveland	GA		10-12-16 S	Std. 0-4-2T		517-519
	Watson-Flandreaux & Co. Groveland		GA	11-29-17			
	Paxton Lumber Corp. Groveland		GA	7-12-20			
	Fender Lumber Co. Jasper		FL	3-12-26			
101430	McKinney & Bennett #8 Westminster	SC		11-14-16 S	Std. 0-4-0T		526-528, 535
101431	Anniston Steel Co. #1 Anniston	AL		12-14-16 S	30" 0-4-0T		544
	Northern Ore Co. Easton		PA	6-20-18			
101432	Norfolk Carolina Timber Corp. #4 Lewiston	NC		3-16-17 O	36" 2-6-0	Mill destroyed by fire, 1920.	567-572
	Stave & Timber Corp. Wallaceton		VA	7-19-21			
	Major & Loomis Co. Pinetown		NC	8-28-26			
101433	Munger & Bennett #9 New Bern	NC		7-28-17 S	Std. 2-6-0	Unit shipped to Newport, NC	601, 604
101434	Central Fortuna Alquizar, Cuba	*		11-5-17 S	30" 0-4-4F		596-598, 626
101435	Pierpont Mfg. Co. #3 Savannah	GA		4-30-20 S	Std. 2-6-0	Engine still in service, May 1942	813
101436	Avent, R.C. #10 Mobile	AL		2-12-24 S	Std. 2-6-0		39
101437	Walker-Jordan Lumber Co. Scotts Ferry	FL		9-1-24 S	Std. 2-6-0		J1, J2

BUILDER'S NUMBER	OWNER(S) & ROAD NUMBER	ORIG. OWNER	SUBSEQ. OWNERS	DATE S = SHIPPED O = ORDERED	GAUGE & TYPE	REMARKS	GLASS PLATE #
	Calhoun-McClellan Lumber Co. Wilma		FL	4-17-28			
	Carter, R.G. Kinard		FL	4-22-31			
	St. Joe Lumber #1 Port St. Joe		FL	0-0-34			
101438	McNeil Coal Co. Brookwood	AL		10-4-22 S	36" 0-4-0T		860
	Black Diamond Coal Mining Co. Brookwood		AL	5-4-23			
101439	Edgar Bros. McIntyre	GA		10-12-23 O	36" 0-4-0	In use April, 1939 as stationary boiler supplying steam to several hoisting engines.	886
101440	Chattahoochee Brick Co. #44 Chattahoochee	GA		4-19-30 S	36" 0-4-0	The last Glover locomotive constructed	
10161	Mexican Sugar Refing Co. #1 Alvarado, Mexico	*		1-3-05 S	36" 0-6-0		361, 362, 363, 365, 387
	Ingenio Santa Fe Tlacotalpam, Jeracruz, Mexico		*	5-16-11			
10162	(Same as 10161)						
	(Same as 10161)						
10163	Cherokee Brick Co. Macon	GA		1-14-05 S	Std. 0-4-0T		
	Burton, E.P. Lumber Co. Charleston		SC	2-1-12			
	Colleton Mercantile & Mfg. Co. Ravanel		SC	4-9-25			
10164	Avent, R.C. #6			10-15-09 S	Std. 0-6-0	File missing	40
10165	Butler, G.F. #10 Knoxville	MS		3-0-10 S	Std. 0-4-0		69, 139
	Arkansas Logging Co. Memphis		TN	2-29-12		Unit at Jarbo spur (Lorays), AK. Arkansas Logging became Lorays Timber Co.	
10166	Williams, F.B. Cypress Co. #47 Patterson	LA		1-23-11 S	Std. 0-6-0		136
	Hartburg Lumber Co. Hartburg		TX	1-8-23			
10167	Roper, John L. Lumber Co. #34 Norfolk	VA		6-27-17 S	36" 2-4-0		591-593
	Baird, David, Jr. Claremont		VA	6-8-25			
10168	McNeill, H.J. Springfield	SC		2-4-25 S	Std. 2-6-0		J6, J7
	Edisto Hardwood Co. Springfield		SC	3-10-28			

BUILDER'S NUMBER	OWNER(S) & ROAD NUMBER	ORIG. OWNER	SUBSEQ. OWNERS	DATE S = SHIPPED O = ORDERED	GAUGE & TYPE	REMARKS	GLASS PLATE #
	Holly Hill Cypress Co. Holly Hill		SC	3-30-38		Still in service, April 1954	
	Richard Stebelton Columbus		OH	8-0-91		Being operated on compressed air on private property as of 1995	
10169	Clinchfield Portland Cement Corp. #1 Clinchfield	GA		12-1-24 O	36" 0-4-0T	File missing, build sheets only. Build sheet shows Coreen, GA. No record of "Coreen"	J3, 4, 5
11161	Wright, A&C #2 Atlanta	GA		0-0-05	36" 0-6-0T		378, 386
11162	Waccama Land & Lumber #1 Bolton	NC		2-2-05 O	Std. 0-4-2T	Forney type with saddle tank	369, 377
11163	Chambers Contracting Co. #2 Macon	GA		9-10-07 S	Std. 0-6-0		41
	Cleveland Oconee Lumber Oconee		GA	0-0-0			
	Carteret Lumber Co. Beaufort		SC	9-7-17			610, 611
11164	Avent, R.C. #5 Leaf	MS		12-7-07 S	Std. 0-6-0		48
	Garbutt, R.M. Register		GA	0-0-0			
	Langford & Ellis Lumber Co. Ridgeland		SC	7-2-29			
11165	Lane Bros. Co. #39 Jackson	GA		6-0-09 S	Std. 0-4-0T	Unit at Ocmulgee Dam	15, 20, 21, 22, 25
	Reynolds, W.H. Construction Co. Braxton		WV	6-10-14			
	Lake Shore Sand & Gravel Erie		PA	3-5-18		Unit at Northeast, PA. Last record in file: 1927	
11166	Hebard Cypress Co. #3 Waycross	GA		1-12-10 S	Std. 2-6-0		42-47
11167	Munger & Bennett #7 New Bern	NC		4-24-11	36" 2-6-0		
11168	Howze Lumber Co. #5 Howze	MS		10-6-11 S	Std. 2-6-0		216
	Cochran Lumber Co. Toinette		AL	1-20-13			
	Lindsey Lumber & Export Co. Mobile		AL	5-5-22			
12161	Garysburg Mfg. Co. #5 Burgaw	NC		5-30-10 S	36" 2-6-0		233
12162	Due West Railway #3 Due West	SC		5-0-10 S	Std. 0-6-0		231, 232
12163	Clear Creek Lumber Co. #1 Reeves	LA		8-31-10 S	Std. 2-6-0		228
	Tulane Lumber Co. Orange		TX	6-7-18		Name changed to Burrus Lumber Co. April, 1920	

BUILDER'S NUMBER	OWNER(S) & ROAD NUMBER	ORIG. OWNER	SUBSEQ. OWNERS	DATE S = SHIPPED O = ORDERED	GAUGE & TYPE	REMARKS	GLASS PLATE #
	Oldham Bros. Orange		TX	3-26-24			
12164	Cartersville RR Co. Cartersville	SC		7-11-11 S	Std. 2-6-0	Cartersville RR Co. owned by Carter & Evans Lumber Co., Cartersville SC	213
	Bell Lumber Co. Marion		SC	8-15-17			
12165	Graves Bros. Lumber Co. #1 Hosford	FL		5-31-11 S	Std. 2-6-0		83, 205, 214, 218, 219, 243
12166	Mayo Lumber Co. #3 McDavid	FL		8-19-11 S	Std. 2-6-0		59, 277
	W.T. Smith & Sons Timber Holtz		FL	3-1-12			
	Twin Tree Lumber #12 Hopkins		GA	11-22-19		Hopkins P.O. is Waycross, GA	738, 781
12167	Westmoreland Lumber Corp. #7 Green Pond	SC		10-31-11 S	Std. 2-6-0		220
	Hilton Dodge Lumber Co. Green Pond		SC	6-0-12			
	Savannah River Lumber Wiggins		SC	11-14-16			
12168	Cassels Cement Gravel Co. #2 Augusta	GA		1-2-12 S	Std. 0-6-0T	Cassels became Georgia Sand & Gravel 2-25-15	256, 258
	Armour Fertilizer Works Bartow		FL	1-11-19			
	Buchanon, S.T. & Sons Lakeland		FL	9-2-24			
	Florida Public Service Co. Orlando		FL	1-18-27			
	Morris Fertilizer Co. Bartow		FL	0-0-0			
	Sherman, W.C. Lumber Co. (no location)			0-0-0			
	Cornell Young Co. Clewiston		FL	3-19-29			
12169	Town Creek Railroad & Lumber Co. #5 Town Creek	NC		8-7-12 S	Std. 2-6-0		113, 222, 223, 224
	Waccamaw Lumber Co. Bolton		NC	5-10-15			
	Town Creek Lumber Co. Town Creek		NC	1-15-16		Town Creek Lumber Co. destroyed by fire 1-18-21	
	Conway Lumber Co. Conway		SC	5-23-23			
121610	Cherokee Brick Co. #4 Macon	GA		3-12-12 S	Std. 0-6-0T	Lettered "Red D"	65
	Small, A.T. Quarries Holton		GA	2-16-18			

121

BUILDER'S NUMBER	OWNER(S) & ROAD NUMBER	ORIG. OWNER	SUBSEQ. OWNERS	DATE S = SHIPPED O = ORDERED	GAUGE & TYPE	REMARKS	GLASS PLATE #
	Tuxbury, A.C. #8 Charleston		SC	1-22-20		Saddletank removed, now 0-6-0	736, 740
121611	Amalgamated Phosphate Co. Chicora	FL		9-6-12 S	Std. 0-6-0T	Name changed to American Cyanamid Co. 8-30-17	254, 255, 257
	Fennel, G.W. Walterboro		SC	2-8-20			
	Thayer Mfg. Co. Walterboro		SC	4-0-20			
121612	Florida Tie & Lumber Co. #102 Jacksonville	FL		1-23-13 S	Std. 2-6-0		109, 111
	Alworth, F.C. Lumber Green Cove Springs		FL	9-16-18			
	Putnam Lumber Co. Bonds Mill		FL	3-21-29			
121613	Twiggs, A.J. & Son Contractors #37 Augusta	GA		2-17-13 S	Std. 0-6-0T		
	Yaryan Rosin & Turpentine #3 Brunswick		GA	3-0-16			
	Hercules Powder Co. Brunswick		GA	1-21-22			
121614	Cherokee Brick Co. #5 Macon	GA		1-28-13 S	Std. 0-6-0T	Unit lettered "S.T.C."	114, 252
	Small, A.T. Quarries Co. Holton		GA	4-7-17			
	Morris, A.G. Stone Co. Holton		GA	5-13-24			
	Macon Crushed Granite Co. Holton		GA	9-16-26			
121615	Amalgamated Phosphate Co. #8 Chicora	FL		4-15-13 S	Std. 0-6-0T		248
121616	Anderson, David O. #2 Marion	SC		7-3-13 S	Std. 2-6-0		112, 225
	Camp Mfg. Co. Whaleyville		VA	0-0-0			
121617	Middleburg Lumber Co. #1 Middleburg	FL		4-7-13 S	Std. 0-6-0		122
	Causey, S.R.. Durbin		FL	10-4-15			
	Cummer Lumber Co. Jacksonville		FL	3-22-16			
	Wilson Cypress Co. Palatka		FL	4-30-18		Still in service, March, 1939	
121618	Great Eastern Lumber Co. #3 Hiltonia	GA		9-9-13 S	Std. 2-6-0		3, 110, 151
	Port Wentworth Lumber Co. Hiltonia		GA	6-26-16			

BUILDER'S NUMBER	OWNER(S) & ROAD NUMBER	ORIG. OWNER	SUBSEQ. OWNERS	DATE S = SHIPPED O = ORDERED	GAUGE & TYPE	REMARKS	GLASS PLATE #
	Union Cypress Co. Hopkins		FL	4-8-25			
121619	Powell Lumber Co. #5 Lake Charles	LA		7-14-13 S	Std. 2-6-0		117, 149, 273, 274
	Bernice Lumber Co. Bernice		LA	10-29-20			
121620	Peavy-Byrnes Lumber Co. #103 Kinder	LA		11-17-13 S	Std. 2-6-0	Operating unit: Kinder & Northwestern Railroad, tender lettered "Little Walter Jasper"	187
121621	Pawnee Land & Lumber Co. #103 Pawnee	LA		2-9-14 S	Std. 2-6-0	Tender lettered "The Little Melvin"	60, 177
	Johnson, H.H. Lumber Co. Haughton		LA	9-7-22			
121622	Danville Lumber & Mfg. Co. #1 Danville	VA		4-25-14 S	Std. 2-6-0		180, 181
	Carteret Lumber Co. Beaufort		NC	7-19-16			
	Brownlee-Lowry Lumber Co. Selma		AL	6-15-25			
121623	Lodwick Lumber Co. #4 Shreveport	LA		4-30-14 S	Std. 2-6-0	Lettered "Kingston RR"	
	Collwood Lumber Co. Lufkin		TX	1-0-20			
	Martin Wagon Co. Veach		TX	9-0-24		Martin Wagon Co. became Kurth Zeagler Lumber Co. September 1925	
121624	Smith, W.T. & Sons Timber Co. #4 Holt	FL		6-12-14 O	Std. 2-6-0	Company bankrupt, 1916	176, 359
	Kanfla Lumber Co. Holt		FL	2-15-17			
	Thayer Mfg. Co. Walterboro		SC	10-19-20			
121625	Burton, E.P. #6 Charleston	SC		8-20-14 O	Std. 2-6-0		167
	West Bay Naval Stores St. Andrews		FL	9-21-16			
	Ehren Pine Co. Ehren		FL	10-24-21			
121626	West Bay Naval Stores St. Andrews	FL		10-23-14 S	Std. 2-6-0	Lettered "Ernest"	322
	Cliffside Railroad Cliffside		NC	9-27-21			
121627	Kentucky Lumber Co. #4 Sulligent	AL		12-22-16 S	Std. 2-6-0		539, 543
	Stover Lumber Co. Wilson		MS	11-21-22			524
121628	Masse & Felton Lumber #3 Macon	GA		5-31-16 S	Std. 2-6-0	Unit offered for sale 3-10-27. No further record.	

BUILDER'S NUMBER	OWNER(S) & ROAD NUMBER	ORIG. OWNER	SUBSEQ. OWNERS	DATE S = SHIPPED O = ORDERED	GAUGE & TYPE	REMARKS	GLASS PLATE #
121629	Prettyman, J.F. & Sons #4 Summerville	SC		4-2-17 S	Std. 2-6-0	Unit offered for sale 4-28-33 and again 6-1-42 as an 0-6-0 at Charleston, SC	561, 562, 575, 576, 580, 582
121630	Lambert, Joseph #9 Littleton	NC		7-2-15 S	36" 2-6-0		444, 444A
	Appomattox Box Shook Co. Petersburg		VA	2-19-17			
	Warsaw Lumber Co. Warsaw		GA	9-23-27		Offered for sale to Glovers 12-20-27 by Maco Lumber Co., Norfolk, VA. Loco at Maco, N.C.	
121631	Empresa Carenero Carenero Venezuela	•		9-21-16 S	36" 0-6-0T		491-498, 500-505, 657
21632	Appomattox Box Shook Co. #2 Kenansville	NC		4-6-17 S	Std. 2-6-0		578, 579
	Blakely Hardwood Co. Blakely		GA	10-22-24			
121633	Cleveland-Oconee Lumber Co. #4 Gardners	GA		7-31-17 S	Std. 2-6-0	Unit still in use, Sept. 1940	614-617, 619, 620
121634	Santa Cecilia Sugar Corp #1 Guantanamo, Cuba	•		2-7-18 S	36" 2-8-0		628, 629, 669, 670, 686
121635	Naval Mine Depot #1 Yorktown	VA		11-0-18 S	Std. 0-4-0T	Unit in use, 1927	701-703
121636	Antofagasra, B.J. #1 Mejillones, Chile	•		11-26-18 S	30" 0-4-2T	Brokered by Nash & Watjen	
121637	Ingenio San Carlos Guayaquil, Ecquador	•		4-16-19 S	42" 2-6-0	Exported by W.R. Grace & Co., N.Y., N.Y. Lettered "San Carlos"	677
121638	Santa Cecilia Sugar Corp. #2 Guantanamo, Cuba	•		12-0-19 S	36" 2-8-0	Unit still in use, Oct., 1936	726, 750, 787
121639	Twin Tree Lumber Co. #11 Hopkins	GA		1-30-20 S	Std. 2-6-0		2, 730, 796
	Cleveland Oconee Lumber Co. Gardners		GA	11-0-26		Unit still in use, April 1937	150, 229, 230
121640	Prettyman, J.F. & Sons #7 Summerville	SC		10-8-20 O	Std. 2-6-0		820, 826
	Huntley-Richardson Lumber Bucksport		SC	9-14-33			
121641	Anderson Lumber Corp. #4 Marion	SC		2-16-23 O	Std. 2-6-0	Company out of business, Jan. 1930	872-875, 884
121642	White Lake Lumber Co. #6 Garland	NC		1-31-23 S	Std. 2-6-2	Unit for sale, Nov. 1927	876, 883
121643	Stover Lumber Co. #5 Mobile	AL		0-0-0	Std. 2-6-2	Unit at Wilson, MS	878
	Ralph Lumber Co. Bolling		AL	1-0-29			
121644	No record of unit being built					No build sheets/no correspondence file	
121645	Serralles, Succesion J. Ponce, Puerto Rico	•		11-12-25 S	39⅜" 2-6-2	In service, April 1942	

BUILDER'S NUMBER	OWNER(S) & ROAD NUMBER	ORIG. OWNER	SUBSEQ. OWNERS	DATE S = SHIPPED O = ORDERED	GAUGE & TYPE	REMARKS	GLASS PLATE #
	Wirshing, George San Truce, Puerto Rico			0-0-0			
13181	Hamilton Ridge Lumber Corp. #1 Estill	SC		5-6-13 S	Std. 2-6-0		148, 226
	Rose, W.P. Supply Co. Columbia		SC	5-0-30			
13182	Econfena Lumber Co. #1 Boyd	FL		1-28-14 S	Std. 2-6-0		235, 245
	Standard Lumber Co. Live Oak		FL	7-23-17			
	Zenoria Lumber Co. Zenoria		LA	8-27-21			
	Standard Lumber Co. Live Oak		FL	11-24-23			
13183	Rock Creek Lumber Co. Hampton Springs	FL		2-18-14 S	Std. 2-6-0		188, 190, 237
	Standard Lumber Co. Live Oak		FL	6-0-17			
13184	Mayo Lumber Co. #1, Milton	FL		7-9-14 S	Std. 2-6-0		
	McGowin Mill Co. Milton		FL	6-0-10		Rebuilt by Glover Jan. 1921	
	Zenoria Lumber Co. Zenoria		LA	4-15-21			825
13185	Jarratt Lumber Co. Marianna	FL		10-28-15 S	Std. 2-6-0		321, 446
	Fitchette & Fitchette Marianna		FL	12-24-19			
	Penn-Jarratt Lumber Co. Marianna		FL	8-24-20			
	May Lumber Co. Marianna		FL	7-10-22			
	Gudenrath Lumber Co. Marianna		FL	9-20-22			
	Tallahassee Lumber Co. Marianna		FL	12-31-25			
	Zenoria Lumber Co. (location not given)			4-28-28			
13186	Cherokee Brick Co. #6 Macon	GA		12-12-16 S	Std. 0-6-0T	Unit still in service, August 1947	536-538
13187	Sondheimer, E. & Co. #411 Sondheimer	LA		4-16-17 O	Std. 2-6-0	Lettered "L.P.T. & W. Ry" (Lake Providence, Texarkana & Western)	563-566, 584, 585
13188	Samana & Santiago #4 Sanchez, Dominican Republic	*		9-0-19 S	42" 2-6-2T	Exported by W.R. Grace Co., N.Y., N.Y.	754, 782-785, 798
13189	Samana & Santiago #5 Sanchez, Dominican Republic			9-0-19 S	42" 2-6-2T	Exported by W.R. Grace Co., N.Y., N.Y.	754, 755

BUILDER'S NUMBER	OWNER(S) & ROAD NUMBER	ORIG. OWNER	SUBSEQ. OWNERS	DATE S = SHIPPED O = ORDERED	GAUGE & TYPE	REMARKS	GLASS PLATE #
131810	Cherokee Brick Co. #7 Macon	GA		1-22-20 S	Std. 0-6-0T	Now at Agrirama, Tifton, GA	733A, 733B
131811	Anderson Lumber Co. South Marion	SC		4-13-20 S	Std. 2-6-0		
131812	Cherokee Brick Co. #8 Macon	GA		5-25-20 S	Std. 0-6-0T	Now at Agrirama, Tifton, GA	735
131813	Tuxbury, A.C. Lumber Co. #9 Charleston	SC		6-12-20 S	Std. 0-6-0	Unit in service 1936	741, 802, 803
131814	Massee & Felton Lumber Co. #4 Adams Park	GA		4-6-20 O	Std. 2-6-0		451, 722, 774
	Osceola Cypress Co. Osceola		FL	4-0-26			
131815	Kunhardt & Co. #1 (no location given)			6-11-20 O	42" 0-6-0T	Exported by J.M. Motley	757, 758, 760, 779, 780
131816	Kunhardt & Co. #2 (no location given)			6-11-20 O	42" 0-6-0T	Exported by J.M. Motley	759, 760, 761, 764
131817	Southern Lumber Co. #5 Savannah	GA		5-23-21 S	Std. 2-6-0		821-823, 827
	Hendrix Mill & Lumber Estill		SC	12-13-39			
131818	Cliffside Railroad Co. #18 Cliffside	NC		7-27-23 S	Std. 2-6-2T	In service, April 1937	868, 869, 871A
14201	Tampa & Northern (no location given)			10-0-06	Std. 4-6-0		366, 367
14202	Interstate Lumber Co. #1 Columbus	MS		6-1-08 S	Std. 4-6-0		107, 402
	Columbus Lumber Co. Columbus		MS	10-0-13			
14203	Peavy-Byrnes Lumber Co. #101 Kinder	LA		8-3-10 S	Std. 4-6-0	Lettered "Kinder & Northwestern Railroad"	97-99, 105, 170
	Peavy-Moore Lumber Co. Deweyville		TX	3-15-26			
14204	Peavy-Byrnes Lumber Co. #102 Kinder	LA		2-3-11 S	Std. 4-6-0	Lettered "Kinder & Northwestern Railroad"	104
	Grand Lake Lumber Co. Conroe		TX	9-25-23			
	Grogen-Cochrane Lumber Co. Tamina		TX	12-5-25			
14205	Wilmington, Brunswick & Southern RR Co. #100 Wilmington	NC		7-13-12 S	Std. 4-6-0		
	Perdido Lumber Co. Millview		FL	11-17-15			
	Russ & McCaskill Barrineau Park		FL	3-26-20			
	Carrollton & Worthville RR Co. Carrollton		KY	10-30-24			

BUILDER'S NUMBER	OWNER(S) & ROAD NUMBER	ORIG. OWNER	SUBSEQ. OWNERS	DATE S = SHIPPED O = ORDERED	GAUGE & TYPE	REMARKS	GLASS PLATE #
14206	Union Cypress Co. #3 Melbourne	FL		9-27-13 S	Std. 2-6-0		3-6, 9, 10, 175
	Arlo Box Co. Oak		FL	1-20-20			
14207	Appomattox Box Shook Co. #1 Petersburg	VA		4-16-14 S	Std. 2-6-0	Lettered "Southern Timber & Land"	357
	Lindsey Lumber Co. Pollard		AL	5-20-16			
	Nixon Smith Construction Montgomery		AL	12-5-20		Utilized for highway construction, Western Louisiana	
	Collwood Lumber Co. Veach		TX	8-14-22		See data, #121623	
14208	Fosburgh Lumber Co. #16 Vaughn	NC		7-18-16 S	Std. 2-6-0		513, 515, 577
	Hollister Lumber Co. Hollister		NC	3-8-20			
	Allied Sand & Gravel Petersburg		VA	1-27-30			
14209	Prettyman, J.F. & Sons #5 Summerville	SC		6-27-17 S	Std. 2-6-0		589, 590
	Schroeder Mills & Timber Co. Pakesley Station, Ontario, Canada		*	12-0-20		Unit still in use, 1930	
142010	Haitian American Sugar Corp. #1 Port-Au-Prince, Haiti	*		10-31-17 S	30" 2-6-0	Lettered "HASCO" In service, July, 1940	607, 612, 613, 624, 644
142011	P.P. Demidoff's Count San Donato Mining & Iron Works Petrograd, Russia	*		10-16-20 S	34.8" 2-8-0	Letter from exporter dated 10-13-20 states, "locomotives to sail from Port of Philadephia aboard S.S. Lordship Manor."	682-685, 775-778, 786
142012	P.P. Demidoff's Count San Donato Mining & Iron Works Petrograd, Russia	*		10-16-20 S	34.8" 2-8-0	Letter from exporter dated 10-13-20 states, "locomotives to sail from Port of Philadephia aboard S.S. Lordship Manor."	
142013	Naval Ammunition Depot, St. Julian's Creek	VA		0-0-18	0-4-0T	Gauge Unknown	648, 652, 659, 660
	Naval Ammunition Depot, Hingham		MA	3-24-40		In service, April 1941	
14221	U.S. Navy Puget Sound	WA		1-18-18 S	Std. 0-4-0		622, 623, 630, 631, 676, 743
	Howard Terminal Co. Oakland		CA	12-0-44			
15201	Haitian American Sugar Corp. #2 Port-Au-Prince, Haiti	*		8-8-18 S	30" 2-6-2	Lettered "HASCO" in service Sept. 1940	645-647, 654, 661, 689, 745, 801A
15202	Haitian American Sugar Corp. #3 Port-Au-Prince, Haiti	*		8-8-18 S	30" 2-6-2	Lettered "HASCO" in service Sept. 1940	801B
15203	Haitian American Sugar Corp. #4 Port-Au-Prince, Haiti	*		0-0-0	30" 2-6-2	Lettered "HASCO" in service July 1940	739, 858, 859
15204	Antioquia Commercial Corp.#3 Buena Ventura, Colombia	*		3-19-18 S	36" 2-6-0	Cab lettered "PAEZ", tender lettered "Ferrocarril De Caldas"	641, 643, 656, 673, 674, J8
16201	Graves Lumber Co. #2 Hosford	FL		1-17-11 S	Std. 4-6-0	Locomotive shipped to Bainbridge, GA. In 1912, replacement parts being shipped to Hosford, FL	32, 102, 103

Index

Agrirama Museum, 31, 45
Alabama Construction Company, 34
Anderson Lumber Corporation, 45
Bon Air Coal & Iron Company, 17
Boyle, J.P., 109
Butler Street Yard, 20
Cameron Lumber Company, 39
Carden Coal Company, 33, 34
Chattahoochee Brick Company, 13, 39
Cherokee Brick Company, 45, 105
Cincinnati, Flemingsburg & Southeastern Railway Co., 17
Cliffside Railroad, 45, 46
Cook Jellico Coal Company, 35
Coulbourn Brothers Lumber Co., 35, 36
Due West Railway Company, 41, 42
Edisto Hardwood Company, 39
Edna Brass Manufacturing Co., 16
Edward Hines Lumber Co., 16
Etna Steel & Iron Company, 107
Eusebia, 32, 33
Ferrell, Mallory Hope, 7
Foster, J.Z., 34
Glover, Aimee Dunwody, 106
Glover, John Heyward, Jr., 8, 9
Glover, James Bolan II, 9
Glover, James Bolan III, 106
Glover, James Bolan IV, 4, 8
Glover, James Bolan V, 4, 8
Graves Lumber Company, 46
Haitian American Sugar Company, 46
Hamby, Ersie, 35
Harris Foundry & Machine Co., 16
Holly Hill Cypress, 39
Johnson, Robert, 25
Lake Shore Sand & Gravel, 41
Lane Brothers Company, 40
Lanier, Alton, 7
Lathrop, David, 5, 36
Lawson, Tom, 7, 110
Lodwick Lumber Company, 43
Log skidder, 10
McNeill, H.J., 39
Mitchell Amusement Company, 16
Mizelle Logging Company, 38
Motley, J.W., 32, 46, 47, 108
Munger & Bennett Lumber Company, 38
NC&StL, 4
O'Toole, Martin K., 5
Phoenix Foundry and Machine Shop, 18
Pickens, Ray, 35
Porter, H.K., 26, 29, 30
Reynolds Coal Company, 33
Samana and Santiago Railway, 33
Six Gun Territory, 39
Splint Jellico Coal Company, 34
Standard Brick Company, 44, 45
Star Head Light Co., 17
Stebelton, Richard, 40
Stratton Brick Company, 11, 105
Welsh, George, 32
Withers family, 18
Woodward Wight Company, 42, 43